The
GREEN POLITICS

Derek Wall

'Publishers have created lists of short books that discuss the questions that your average [electoral] candidate will only ever touch if armed with a slogan and a soundbite. Together [such books] hint at a resurgence of the grand educational tradition... Closest to the hot headline issues are *The No-Nonsense Guides*. These target those topics that a large army of voters care about, but that politicos evade. Arguments, figures and documents combine to prove that good journalism is far too important to be left to (most) journalists.'

Boyd Tonkin,
The Independent,
London

About the author
Derek Wall is a green activist, writer and economist. He was the last male Principal Speaker of the Green Party of England and Wales. He teaches New Radical Political Economy at Goldsmiths College, University of London. He has written a number of books on green economics and politics including *Earth First! and the Anti-Roads Movement* (Routledge, 1999) and *Babylon and Beyond* (Pluto, 2005). He has a newspaper column with the *Morning Star*. A lifelong ecosocialist, he blogs at http://another-green-world.blogspot.com/

Acknowledgements
Chris Brazier is wonderful to work with as a patient editor. Amanda Fallows and Phil Wilson have done a tremendous job supporting me as a Green Party General Election candidate, giving me time to complete this book. Thanks to all the contributors to the foreword and special thanks to Nandor Tanczos and Brent McMillan for reading early drafts and providing feedback. The mistakes are all mine!

The **NO-NONSENSE GUIDE** to

GREEN POLITICS

Derek Wall

BTL

The No-Nonsense Guide to Green Politics

Published in Canada by
New Internationalist™ Publications Ltd.   and   Between the Lines
2446 Bank Street, Suite 653   720 Bathurst Street, Suite 404
Ottawa, Ontario   Toronto, Ontario
K1V 1A8   M5S 2R4
www.newint.org   **www.btlbooks.com**

First published in the UK by
New Internationalist™ Publications Ltd
55 Rectory Road
Oxford OX4 1BW
New Internationalist is a registered trade mark.

© Derek Wall/New Internationalist 2010

Series editor: Chris Brazier
Design by New Internationalist Publications Ltd

Printed by T J International Limited, Cornwall, UK
who hold environmental accreditation ISO 14001.

Mixed Sources
Product group from well-managed
forests and other controlled sources
www.fsc.org Cert no. SGS-COC-2482
© 1996 Forest Stewardship Council

FSC

Library and Archives Canada Cataloguing in Publication

Wall, Derek
The no-nonsense guide to green politics / Derek Wall.

(No-nonsense guides)
Includes bibliographical references and index.
ISBN 978-1-897071-68-7

1. Political ecology. 2. Green movement. 3. Environmentalism.
I. Title. II. Series: No-nonsense guides (Toronto, Ont.)
JA75.8.W35 2010   304.2   C2010-901110-4

Between the Lines gratefully acknowledges assistance for its publishing
activities from the Canada Council for the Arts, the Ontario Arts Council, the
Government of Ontario through the Ontario Book Publishers Tax Credit program
and through the Ontario Book Initiative, and the Government of Canada through
the Book Publishing Industry Development Program.

 Canada   Canada Council
for the Arts   Conseil des Arts
du Canada   ONTARIO ARTS COUNCIL
CONSEIL DES ARTS DE L'ONTARIO

Foreword

The No-Nonsense Guide to Green Politics gives the lie to the idea that Green parties worldwide are concerned only with the environment. Derek Wall's fascinating book shows the deep roots of green politics in the struggles for peace and social justice as well as ecology. It also draws out the worldwide connections that make us strong.

All over the world, Green Party members are working as elected national representatives – though unfortunately not yet in the US. More than 20 years ago in my country, Green Party members saw through the sham of a political system based on two major parties appearing to serve the interests of ordinary people while actually serving the special interests that include some ideological, corporate and military élites. My presidential campaign was a step towards the US Green Party being recognized as the legitimate third party – and at long last providing a voice for those who suffer from the lack of a living wage, from the erosion of civil liberties, from the refusal to provide universal healthcare, from the insistence on waging interminable war, and from the reckless pursuit of profit at all costs, even at the expense of the earth.

This book underscores the values shared by Green movement campaigners all over the world – at the same time as sketching out the difficulties we will inevitably face as we seek to see our values prevail in public policy.

Cynthia McKinney,
Green Party candidate in the
2008 US presidential election

Derek Wall has provided an inspiring introduction to green politics. His *No-Nonsense Guide* underlines the need for both ecological politics and social justice. A member of the Green Party here in England and Wales since 1980, his book is shaped by his activism as an

5

election candidate, former Green Party Principal Speaker and his commitment to nonviolent direct action.

Green politics is vital if we are to have a sustainable and happy future. This book outlines key green ideas from notions of animal rights to the Green New Deal. Faced, as we are, with the threat of climate change, financial catastrophe and peak oil, green politics is more relevant than ever.

Far from being about austerity and sacrifice, green politics are about creating an economy that delivers prosperity in the long term. The Green New Deal, for example, is a way of reducing our dependency on increasingly expensive and scarce oil, while creating jobs in renewable energy and promoting reform of the financial system. Localizing the economy will mean greater democratic control, fresher food and a reduced impact on fragile ecosystems.

Green politics is about considering the needs of future generations. The Green Party in the UK has evolved to the point where its members can be elected at all levels of the political system. *The No-Nonsense Guide to Green Politics* will help contribute to the growth not just of green parties but a wider green movement both in the UK and globally.

Caroline Lucas,
Green Party Member in the European Parliament and leader of the Green Party of England and Wales

The agenda of the international green movement will dominate the next century, as the demands of the labor movement (and the responses of capitalism to them) dominated the last. What that agenda is, its boundaries and dynamics, remains fluid although its broad thrust is clear. In this book Derek Wall sets out the foundations of green philosophy as it has spontaneously developed in various places around the world, as well as articulating the major points of debate and disagreement. In doing so, he has made green political ideas more accessible and understandable to a general audience.

Importantly, Derek does not shy away from the most contentious arguments that have riven some green organizations. The question of whether green politics is left politics has caused considerable tension at times and continues to resurface in Green parties to this day. The nature of the state and how far green solutions rely on empowering the nation-state is also fiercely debated in a movement that has brought together a number of divergent strands of activists, from unionists to anarchists to first nations. Finally, the question of whether the international structures of global capitalism, such as the World Trade Organization and the World Bank, can be reformed or need to be replaced has been a crucial point of difference in international green forums. The same question, of course, can be applied to corporate capitalism itself.

Derek Wall is well placed to write such a book. He has played a number of important roles in the Green Party of England and Wales and continues to stand in general elections. He is involved in campaigning on a number of green issues, and is active in the ongoing debates that continue to shape the green movement worldwide. He brings a well-informed and critical analysis to the project, making this a valuable contribution to the green library.

Nándor Tánczos,
former Green Party MP in
New Zealand/Aotearoa

The world is changing and challenging us, and people are changing too. Maybe not as fast as we need, unfortunately not as fast as the world for sure, but there have been important processes of political convergence in the last few years worldwide. Many different strands are now pushing for a change of paradigm, aiming to build a human society that makes peace with nature and with itself, not leaving anybody behind and preserving the ecosystems that support life on Earth.

The green movement in general – represented by the Green parties in Europe, or by the Political Ecology networks in Latin America, to give just two examples – has been part of this struggle for many years, but there have been many misunderstandings regarding its approach to achieving the vision of a healthy environment and at the same time guaranteeing a dignified life for millions of poor people on the planet.

But politics is the art of the possible. New alliances are forming, we have been too separated for too long, and those fighting for people's rights, for healthy food, for social change and for nature, are trying to find a common platform to face powerful economic interests and privileged élites that are well positioned in governments worldwide.

Common sense is not as common as it should be – and unfortunately is very scarce in politics. *The No-Nonsense Guide to Green Politics* makes a modest but important contribution to finding that common sense and spreading it. Derek Wall's interesting book shows us about strategy and struggle and how to fight for the environment is to fight for the people. A better world is possible.

Roberto Pérez Rivero,
Cuban sustainability activist

CONTENTS

Introduction

MY FIRST ENCOUNTER with green politics was back in 1979 when I was 14. I was interested in politics and the environment and it happened that my next-door neighbors were hosting an Ecology Party meeting – they were wardens of the Almshouse in the small Wiltshire town of Corsham, where I lived. I went along. It was heady stuff. The schoolroom of the Almshouse contained a pulpit from which Patrick Rivers, a former civil servant who had dropped out and embraced radical ecology, virtually delivered a sermon. I guess if I had lived somewhere else I might never have got involved.

1979 is a long time ago but Rivers, a charismatic figure, talked of environmental destruction, alienating consumerism and the threat of nuclear war. I was fascinated. I joined the Ecology Party, which went through thin times during the early 1980s and nearly disappeared before reinventing itself as the Green Party in 1985. Today, green politics is a worldwide phenomenon, Green parties have participated in coalition government in many European countries, and threats to the environment such as climate change are always in the news.

At 14, I was interested in animal liberation issues such as factory farming, fox hunting and the bloody Japanese dolphin culls. I was skeptical that the economy could keep on expanding, with more production, consumption and waste, without wrecking the planet's ecosystems. I still am.

Every day, the issue of how we get to a green society that works ecologically, is socially just and democratic, haunts me. I have written more words than I like to think of, delivered many leaflets, contested numerous election campaigns, have taken part in nonviolent direct action, have worked to get indigenous activists out of prison and much else besides.

What could be more important than green politics? Green politics is the politics of survival, yet the way we live in a capitalist society that seemingly can only dance to the drumbeat of profit, threatens everything. Moving to a world where humanity can prosper without wrecking the environment is a vital necessity but sometimes seems impossibly difficult.

There are inevitably contradictions – green politics has become more mainstream but as Greens have been elected, they have risked having their radical edge blunted by compromises with the powers-that-be. Green parties have emerged, grown and influenced society but the message of green politics has also been taken forward by radical direct action campaigns such as the climate camp, by indigenous social movements, and by politicians such as Bolivia's President Evo Morales.

Today I work with Green politicians like Caroline Lucas here in Britain and indigenous leaders like the legendary Hugo Blanco in Peru. I am both pessimistic and optimistic. The more we learn about climate change, the more urgent change seems, yet the governments of the world seem unable to meet the challenge. I am optimistic that an alternative is possible, one led by people at the grassroots.

Real economic development, political participation and ecological sanity are all aspects of green politics that are becoming a reality. Some 30 years after my first encounter with green politics, I read the news that Elinor Ostrom had won the Nobel Prize for Economics by advocating an ecological economics based on the commons. Perhaps her victory shows that what is necessary is no longer impossible.

Derek Wall
Windsor, England,
March 2010

1 Global green politics

The term 'green politics' was once synonymous with the German Greens, who have participated in governments for much of the last three decades. But Green parties have now gone global – from Kenya to Mongolia, Taiwan to Brazil. And green political activity encompasses non-electoral campaigns and direct-action techniques the world over.

IN 1983, 28 MEMBERS of the German Green Party were elected to the West German parliament. Dressed informally in jeans, some of them brought in plants to place on their desks. Their colorful arrival contrasted with the suited members from the traditional parties.

Their success marked the first entry into a national parliament of a group of greens. The German Greens were elected in 1983 on a platform with four key elements: ecology, social justice, peace and grassroots democracy.

Green parties were born in the early 1970s, grew in the 1980s and green politics is now a global phenomenon. Green politics is first and foremost the politics of ecology; a campaign to preserve the planet from corporate greed, so we can act as good ancestors to future generations. However, green politics involves more than environmental concern.

Ecology may be the first pillar of green politics but it is not the only one. Andrew Dobson, an English Green Party member and academic, has argued that green politics is a distinct political ideology. While much ink has been spilt defining the term 'ideology', Dobson argues that it is a set of political ideas rather than a single idea, even one as powerful as concern for the environment. He argues that a political ideology provides a map of reality, which helps to show its adherents how to understand the world. He also believes that ideologies demand the transformation of society. He uses the term 'ecologism' to distinguish green politics from simple 'environmentalism'.

The second pillar of green politics – social justice – is vital. Greens argue that environmental protection should not come at the expense of the poor or lead to inequality. This social justice element places greens on the left of the political spectrum. Greens argue, however, that the right-left spectrum is not the only dimension of politics, not least because there are many political parties that are committed to social justice but which fail to protect nature.

The third pillar – grassroots democracy – also distinguishes greens from many traditional socialists who have often promoted centralized governance of societies. This is a principle that greens share with anarchists and other libertarians. The demand for participatory democracy was one of the most important inspirations behind the German Greens. Greens during the 1980s made strong attempts to function in as decentralist and participatory a fashion as possible. Leaders were rejected, politics based on personality frowned upon and decisions made collectively. In the 21st century, Green parties are less radical but still pride themselves on allowing members to participate in policy and decision-making, even as democracy has gone out of fashion in many other political parties.

Nonviolence is the final pillar. Green parties evolved partly out of the peace movement and oppose war, the arms trade and solutions based on violence. Again, over time this commitment has become a little less clear-cut. The German Greens moved from being a radically anti-war party to participating in a government that sent German forces into Serbia. Greens have compromised over peace by supporting armed liberation movements such as the African National Congress, where they consider that strict nonviolence might lead to continued oppression.

Global green politics

The German Greens under Foreign Minister Joschka Fischer were, however, leading opponents of the 2003 invasion of Iraq.

Green politics does not stop with Green parties; the green movement as a whole is much larger. For example, green direct action networks such as Earth First!, Reclaim the Streets and Climate Camp have emerged in recent decades. These green direct-action networks focus on environmental issues but also promote the other pillars of green politics such as grassroots democracy, nonviolence and opposition to social injustice. Non-governmental organizations (NGOs) such as Greenpeace and Friends of the Earth have, meanwhile, a more ambiguous relationship with green politics. As environmental pressure groups, they lack party political ambition and ideology. Yet they have often worked with more radical direct-action networks and Green parties to achieve political change. Greenpeace has also combined the anti-war and environmental elements of green politics. Many environmental NGOs combine environment concern with promoting social justice and grassroots democracy.

The green movement is a little like an iceberg, with some highly visible Green parties, direct-action groups and radical NGOs looming large above looser and less visible networks of those who practice green lifestyles or contribute more sporadically to political change.

Green history

The origins of green politics are normally traced to the late 1960s and early 1970s. The first ecological political party – Australia's United Tasmania Group – was formed in March 1972 to campaign against a big dam and to preserve the rainforests. Although they received a modest three per cent in state elections and failed in their goal of preserving Lake Pedder, they inspired the creation of Green parties all over the world. Their

charter, a kind of manifesto, noted that they were:
- United in a global movement for survival;
- Concerned for the dignity of humanity and the value of cultural heritage while rejecting any view of humans which gives them the right to exploit all of nature;
- Moved by the need for a new ethic, which unites humans with nature to prevent the collapse of life support systems of the earth.[1]

A few weeks after the launch of the United Tasmania Group, a New Zealand/Aotearoa party called Values was formed at a meeting at Victoria University in Wellington. The Party had strong zero growth, gay rights and drug reform policies. It was the first party in New Zealand/Aotearoa to have a woman leader and an openly gay election candidate. However, in the 1970s, before the introduction of proportional representation, Values found it difficult to make an electoral impact and faded. It did, however, help to keep the country nuclear free and laid the foundations for the present Green Party, which is one of the strongest in the world.

Values and the United Tasmania Group were inspired by reports such as *Limits to Growth* and *Blueprint for Survival*, which argued that humanity was threatening vital ecosystems and depleting resources. *Limits to Growth* was produced by a team of scientists at the Massachusetts Institute of Technology and used computer models to argue that, unless growth ceased, ecological catastrophe would result. The oil crisis of 1973 made such ideas fashionable. *Blueprint for Survival*, based on similar assumptions, was published in Britain by *The Ecologist* magazine, creating a huge public debate.

On 6 December 1973, *The Guardian* reported the birth of a new British party known simply as PEOPLE. Its manifesto stated boldly that it sought 'a transition to a stable society in which people and places matter, which recognizes that the Earth's resources are limited and that we must learn to live as part of nature, not as its master'. PEOPLE became the Ecology Party in 1975 and changed its name again to the Green Party in 1985. Today, it has two Members of the European Parliament, two members of the Greater London Assembly and over a hundred local councilors. The Scottish Green Party currently has two members of the Scottish Parliament.

The German and French Greens were also influenced by an anti-growth agenda. A Christian Democrat member of the West German Parliament, Herbert Gruhl, left his centre-right party to sit as an ecologist in the Bundestag. The French Ecologist presidential candidate René Dumont stressed the no growth agenda in his 1974 election campaign. However, in France and Germany, together with other western European countries, the Greens grew largely out of the movements against nuclear power in the 1970s.

The German Greens, in particular, saw themselves as the electoral wing of a wider protest movement. In fact, they contested elections into the 1980s as a list of candidates rather than as a formal political party, reflecting their social movement connections. The German extra-parliamentary left, which exploded on to the scene in the late 1960s and early 1970s, provided the German Greens with most of their initial key activists, including future Party leader Fischer. The events of Paris in 1968 – where the student demonstrators coined slogans attacking a society obsessed with shopping, such as 'Down with the consumer society, the more you consume, the less you are' – also fed into later developments in green politics.

The counterculture of the 1960s also fed into green party politics and the wider green movement. The counterculture drew on radical thinkers such as Herbert Marcuse and Erich Fromm from the Frankfurt

School. They condemned capitalism not just because it exploited workers but also because it dehumanized us as passive consumers and polluted the environment. Counterculture thinkers of a different ilk, such as Aldous Huxley and Hermann Hesse, also influenced the nascent green politics. Huxley's last novel, the utopia *Island*, provides a green blueprint for many aspects of society, including education, spirituality and the family. Charles Reich's *The Greening of America* and Theodore Roszak's *Where the Wasteland Ends* were also important to the emerging green movement.

While the 1960s counterculture and the 1970s scientific challenge to a growth economy were vital parts of the mix, green politics can be seen as having deeper roots. Peter Gould's book *Early Green Politics* argues that the most 'important period of green politics before 1980 lay between 1880 and 1900'.[2] During this period the socialist, writer and artist William Morris drew upon the romantic ideas of John Ruskin to promote a political agenda that opposed industrial pollution and promoted conservation. Morris, politically active in opposing the Crimean War, also established a group to conserve churches.

Greens in Europe

Green parties' share of the vote and number of MEPs gained in European Parliament Election 2009.

	% of vote	No of MEPs
Luxembourg	17%	1
France	16%	14
Belgium	15%	4
Germany	12%	14
Finland	12%	2
Sweden	11%	3
Austria	10%	2
Netherlands	9%	3
UK	9%	2
Spain	3%	2
Greece	3%	1

Source: www.europaparl.europa.eu

Global green politics

He became interested in Marxism, joined the Social Democratic Federation, Britain's first socialist political party, along with Friedrich Engels and Marx's daughter, Eleanor. Morris worked tirelessly to promote his own version of ecosocialism and wrote a utopian novel – *News from Nowhere* – promoting a green alternative. Gould argues that he was part of a much wider network of socialists and anarchists who shared virtually all the values of the modern green movement. Another prominent early green political activist was Edward Carpenter, in the late 19th and early 20th centuries. An openly gay man, an advocate of feminism and animal rights, he lived in near self-sufficiency with his partner George Merrill and founded the Sheffield Socialist Society. He believed that 'The vast majority of mankind (sic) must live in direct contact with nature.'[3]

Even earlier examples of green politics can be found: the left-wing English Romantic poets such as William Blake and Percy Bysshe Shelley, along with Mary Shelley, come to mind. Indeed the novelist EM Forster described Carpenter as practicing the 'socialism of Shelley and Blake'. Mary Shelley's novel *Frankenstein* is an early piece of eco-literature, critiquing a science that manipulates nature with destructive results and creates a sad monster. The French philosopher Rousseau can, meanwhile, be seen as an early or proto-green who advocated a closer human connection to nature. While global environmental threats from nuclear weapons testing in the 1960s to climate change more recently has led to the growth of green politics, environmental problems have a long history. Indeed, laws against air pollution were enacted in Britain as early as the 13th century.

Green parties go global
Green parties are now a global phenomenon. The most successful African Green party has been the

Mazingira Green Party of Kenya – *mazingira* is the Swahili word for 'environment'. Mazingira's 1997 presidential candidate Wangari Maathai also founded the Green Belt Movement, which encouraged tree planting as a conservation measure. She won a Nobel Prize for her work promoting peace and environmental justice. In 2009 the global federation of Green parties contained 19 members from African countries.

Greens have been elected in Benin and Senegal. There have been several attempts to create Green parties in South Africa, and most recently the Ecopeace Party and a variety of socialist groups based in Soweto have come together to found the Socialist Green Coalition. A Green Party candidate in Burkina Faso received seven per cent of the vote in the 1998 presidential election, while the former left-wing President Thomas Sankara – sadly assassinated – was a keen exponent of environmental policies such as community tree planting.

There are also a number of Green parties in Central and Latin America. The most successful by far has been the Brazilian Green Party (PV). The musician Gilberto Gil, a party member, acted as Minister of Culture in the coalition government. The former Environment Minister Marina Silva is to run as the Green Presidential candidate. Silva, who comes from a family of rubber tappers, has been a passionate defender of the Amazon. The Green Party of Chile is also well established but has not yet managed to elect parliamentarians. In much of Latin America left-leaning governments have become aware of environmental issues and green NGOs have emerged. The contribution of indigenous groups to green politics is particularly important in Latin America. Many Latin American Green parties have a skeletal organization and may represent little more than small groups of individuals with access to websites.

Green parties are relatively weak in North America

as well – there are no Green representatives in the US Congress or the Canadian Parliament. One of the key factors affecting Green parties' electoral success there has been the voting system. Green parties in much of Europe have gained some success because of proportional representation (PR). While PR systems vary, they typically guarantee that, if a political party gains 10 per cent of votes in a national election, it will gain 10 per cent of seats in parliament. Like the UK, Canada and the US have a 'first-past-the post' system, which explains the absence of nationally elected Greens in all three countries – though as this book goes to press the Green Party of England and Wales is confident that it will achieve an historic breakthrough by winning at least one parliamentary seat in the 2010 General Election.

In the US, the highest office achieved by greens so far is that of Mayor. US greens started organizing in the 1980s with a radical decentralist model inspired by the German Greens, as activists established Committees of Correspondence – a reference to revolutionary organization in the 18th-century war of independence against Britain. The Citizens Party, headed by the ecologist Barry Commoner, stood on an essentially green election platform during the 1980s before dissolving. In 1996, the consumer activist Ralph Nader stood as the Green Presidential candidate together with the indigenous activist Winona LaDuke. In 2000, Nader gained three per cent of the national presidential vote but his success led to bitter controversy as Democrats argued that his votes had prevented their candidate Al Gore from beating George W Bush. In 2008 the former US congress member Cynthia McKinney ran for President, together with hip hop artist Rosa Clements. The number of votes gained was modest but the campaign helped to build the party, which held to a platform of 10 key green demands. McKinney has been highly active in promoting conservation and civil rights, and in opposing both nuclear power and Israeli treatment of Palestinians.

The Green Party in Canada was preceded by a group called the Small Party, inspired by EF Schumacher's book on green economics *Small Is Beautiful*. The Party is currently led by Elizabeth May, who is one of Canada's most famous environmentalists. It is proud of its 'neither right nor left' orientation and has shifted from its decentralist and somewhat anarchic roots. Despite much favorable media attention, it has found it difficult to elect members to either the national or state legislatures. There are strong environmental direct action groups and indigenous networks in Canada, currently campaigning against exploitation of the highly polluting tar sands in Alberta.

Asian-Pacific progress

A network of Asian-Pacific Green parties was established in Kyoto, Japan, in 2005 and its full membership includes parties from Australia, New Zealand/Aotearoa, Japan, Pakistan, Korea, Taiwan and New Caledonia, with associates in Nepal, Mongolia and Polynesia.

The Australian Green Party is particularly strong, having won seats both in the Senate and in state assemblies, most significantly in Tasmania. It evolved from the United Tasmania Group and the 1980s Nuclear Disarmament Party and has gradually overtaken the centre-left Democrats. In 2007, the Australian Greens received nine per cent of the vote in national elections and elected five senators, while in 2009 they won the seat of Fremantle in Western Australia with 54 per cent of the vote. They are growing fast. The Socialist Alliance also strongly promotes green policies, not least via the ecosocialist newspaper *Green Left Weekly*.

The Green Party of Aotearoa New Zealand, which

evolved from the earlier Values Party, is also booming. A shake-up in the New Zealand political system in the 1990s saw the creation of the Alliance, a coalition of political parties, which the Greens joined for a time, and the introduction of proportional representation. Both factors helped them gain their first Members of Parliament in the 1996 election and they have since had some influence with Labour governments. They have been strong opponents of GM farming. Currently they have nine members of parliament. The Party has two co-leaders, one of which must be female and one

Green politics in the Middle East

There are a very small number of Green parties in the Middle East. Some, like the Green Party of Saudi Arabia, are underground organizations comprising little more than a website and a few committed individuals. The long-standing Egyptian Green Party typically finds it difficult to progress in a country where democratic participation is limited.

Israel, however, contains two such parties, the new and more radical Green Movement and the Green Party, which has been closer to the Israeli state. There is also a Green Leaf Party committed to cannabis legislation. None have elected parliamentarians, although the Green Party has elected local officials.

The Green Movement narrowly failed to elect members of the Knesset in the 2009 election. It supports a two-state solution to the conflict between Israel and the Palestinians, and campaigns strongly on civil liberties and tolerance to religious difference. It believes that energy consumption in the country should be cut by 25 per cent.

However, green politics is probably best represented by the left party Hadesh. Dov Khenin from Hadesh is co-coordinator of a network of Israeli environmental groups, a member of the Knesset and came second in the 2008 Tel Aviv mayoral election with 34 per cent. Hadesh has opposed Israel's attacks on Gaza and the Lebanon and supports the creation of a Palestinian state.

The Lebanese Green Party, one of the world's newest, campaigns with the slogan 'The earth knows no religion' in a country where most parties have Shi'a, Sunni or Christian affiliations. As well as the pursuit of peace, a particular concern is forest conservation: their chair Christopher Skeff observed that '5,000 years ago a squirrel could travel the whole country by merely hopping from tree to tree'. He also noted: 'I cannot pretend that Lebanese people will rally to us because of our non-confessional status, but I know a lot of them have had enough of sectarianism.' ∎

male – currently Metiria Turei and Russel Norman. The Party has been a keen advocate of law reform on cannabis and managed to put through anti-smacking legislation to protect children. The party made history by achieving the election of the world's first Rastafarian MP, Nándor Tánczos, in 1999. A passionate radical ecologist, when Tánczos left parliament in 2008 he smashed his watch in a symbolic gesture. Concerned that his radical edge would be dulled, he noted: 'The danger is the system changes us as much as we change the system, if not more. And that's why I'm leaving.' He claimed that he did not need his watch. 'When I look at the state of our rivers, our atmosphere and our communities, I don't need a watch to know what time it is.'

The Japanese Green Party came about through a merger between the Rainbow Green network of local groups and the Environmental Green Party. They first gained national electoral success with the victory of Ryuhei Kawad in a Tokyo seat in the Lower House – though, because of the expense and difficulties of registration, he ran as an independent. Infected with HIV via a blood transfusion, he is a well-known campaigner in the country. As a parliamentarian his first act was to visit the Kashiwazaki nuclear power plant, which had been damaged by an earthquake. As well as campaigning against nuclear power, he has worked for patients' rights and protested against Japanese support for the military regime in Burma.

There is an underground Chinese Green Party as well as a Green Party in Taiwan, which has elected local officials but has so far failed to gain national representation. At present there is no national Indian Green Party. But in China, India and much of East Asia, there are vigorous environmental protest movements. Campaigns against dams that displace people and destroy forests have been significant in both China and India. In West Bengal, the ruling Communist Party lost state elections in 2009 after decades of power because of its support for industrialization that led to peasants losing their land. The most controversial case was at Nandigram, where a car factory was built on land taken from local peasants who argued that they had not agreed and were not adequately compensated.

Such protests against land seizures for industrial development are also increasingly common in China. China has seen the emergence of widespread environmental protest as when, in May 2007, students and professors at Xiamen University sent out a million text messages urging citizens to protest against the

Petra Kelly

Despite her opposition to leaders and personality politics, the best-known face of green politics during the 1980s was the German activist Petra Kelly. Born in Bavaria, the most conservative state in the country, Kelly went to study in the US and embraced nonviolence, feminism, environmental concern and a radical style of participatory politics, before helping to launch the German Greens.

She saw herself as part of a tradition that embraced Rosa Luxemburg, Martin Luther King, Gandhi and the suffragettes. She was deeply affected by the death of her sister from cancer, fearing that radioactive emissions and other forms of pollution were leading to the 'cancerization' of the world.

Active in the growing anti-nuclear movement of the 1980s, she coined the phrase 'anti-party party', seeing the Greens as an alternative to traditional party politics in the grey West German system. As well as helping to found the Greens, she was a Green member of parliament and a party speaker.

During the 1980s and early 1990s she was excited by the growth of the Greens but anxious that they were becoming just another political party. Her energy symbolized the potential for green politics to put women at the center. During the 1980s, she became well known in countries as diverse as Australia, India and the US as an inspiring political figure.

She was killed in mysterious circumstances, apparently murdered by her partner Gert Bastian, another Green politician and former General, in 1992. She is still greatly missed today and her book *Fighting for Hope – the Nonviolent Way to a Green Future* continues to inspire activists.

She once noted: 'We, the generation that faces the next century, can add the solemn injunction, "If we don't do the impossible, we shall be faced with the unthinkable".' ∎

proposed construction of a $1.4 billion petrochemical plant; between 7,000 and 20,000 people marched on the resultant demonstration, ignoring threats from the authorities.[4] Chinese Green Party members have argued: 'Environmental sustainability is impossible without social justice, and social justice is impossible without democratic politics.'[5]

The Green Party in neighboring Mongolia is one of the more successful in the region, having elected members of parliament and participated in coalition government. In 2008, its leader, Saruul Agvaandorj, was briefly imprisoned following protests against election irregularities.[6]

Greening Europe

Green parties are strongest in western Europe and have had members in the European Parliament since 1984. They have been able to use their strong position to promote renewable energy, cuts in carbon dioxide emissions, legislation against pesticides and strong social policies. Currently the Green group in the European Parliament is the fourth largest after the centre right, socialist and liberal blocs. It has 55 members, currently including a member of the free software Pirate Party from Sweden.

Green Parties have moved from the margins to the mainstream to participate in coalition governments right across Europe. Paradoxically or not, some of the most notorious radical figures of European politics in the late 1960s, such as Daniel Cohn-Bendit, have become important green realists or moderates.

The German Greens saw a debate in the early and mid-1980s between 'realos' who wished to go into coalition with the Social Democrats and 'fundis', fundamentalists who believed that coalition would lead to compromises and dilute the green message. 'Realos' have tended to favor conventional party structures, while 'fundis' are radical democrats, putting forward the view of the prominent 1980s activist Petra Kelly that the Greens were an 'anti-party party'. The 'fundis' lost the debate and the German Greens soon gained a share of political power. Acting as coalition partners with the Social Democrats, first at a regional level, they helped to govern Germany between 1998 and 2005. The iconic radicalism of the Green Party was rather diluted but they introduced policies to phase out nuclear power and opposed the US invasion of Iraq in 2003. Their leader, Joschka Fischer, moved from being a street activist (closely associated with some of those who drifted into terrorism in the Red Army Faction) to becoming Germany's Foreign Minister and the country's most popular politician.

Belgium, the Czech Republic, France, Ireland, Italy and Sweden have all seen coalition governments involving Green parties in the last decade. Even in the UK, the Greens have had a share of power in the Greater London Assembly, working with Ken Livingstone, the Mayor of London between 1999 and 2008, to introduce the congestion charge on cars using city roads, promote cycling and fight for higher pay for London's workers.

There are also a number of specifically red-green parties and groups. Iceland is currently governed by a coalition between the Green Left Movement and the Socialist Alliance. The Nordic Green Left, meanwhile, is a bloc of left parties, including a number of communist parties, that embrace ecosocialist politics.

The rise of green direct action
Green politics has never been limited to Green parties. It has always had an anarchist element that is skeptical of elected politicians and fears being absorbed by the political system. There are a number of green grassroots networks that reject party politics, one of the most notable of which is Earth First!

Earth First! (EF!) was originally founded in the

US during the 1980s by activists in environmental groups such as the Wilderness Society and the Sierra Club. They felt that existing environmental groups had failed, especially during the years of the right-wing Reagan presidency. Working under the slogan 'No Compromise in Defense of Mother Earth', Earth First!ers advocated direct action, including 'ecotage' (green-themed sabotage), to deal with environmental threats. Some of the individuals involved in EF! put forward what was effectively an extreme right-wing version of deep ecology. Founder member Dave Foreman shockingly argued, for example, that AIDS was beneficial if it cut population levels. EF! was widely criticized by other greens for such opinions. Foreman later recanted his more regressive views and

---

What is green politics?

Jonathon Porritt's criteria for identifying the key elements of green politics:

• A reverence for the Earth and for all its creatures;
• A willingness to share the world's wealth among *all* its peoples;
• Prosperity to be achieved through sustainable alternatives to the rat race of economic growth;
• Lasting security to be achieved through non-nuclear defense strategies and considerably reduced arms spending;
• A rejection of materialism and the destructive values of industrialism;
• A recognition of the rights of future generations in our use of all resources;
• An emphasis on socially useful, personally rewarding work, enhanced by human scale technology;
• Protection of the environment as a precondition of a healthy society;
• An emphasis on personal growth and spiritual development; respect for the gentler side of human nature;
• Open, participatory democracy at every level of society;
• Recognition of the crucial importance of significant reductions in population levels;
• Harmony between people of every race, color and creed;
• A non-nuclear, low-energy strategy, based on conservation, greater efficiency and renewable resources;
• An emphasis on self-reliance and decentralized communities.

Source: Jonathon Porritt *Seeing Green*, Blackwell, London 1987.

activists like Judi Bari moved EF! in a progressive direction, making alliances with workers to tackle environmental threats such as logging.

EF! inspired green direct action in many other parts of the world. The British branch of EF!, which was launched in 1991, became a key part of a campaign to stop a huge program of road building that would have devastated the environment. At Twyford Down in Hampshire, a loose group of new age travelers, local people, Earth First!ers and other greens, used direct action to try to prevent the building of a motorway through an area of natural beauty. They failed – as did protests that mobilized thousands to stop roads in east London, Newbury, Glasgow and elsewhere. However, the government cut the wider road-building program and the green movement in the UK was both energized and radicalized. British EF! activists rejected Dave Foreman's ideas and, with their emphasis on social justice and anti-capitalism, overlapped with an anarchist approach to green politics. They went on to form Reclaim the Streets, an anti-roads movement that held street parties involving thousands of people, aimed at reclaiming roads from the car culture.

With the rise of concern over climate change and a fear that governments will either fail to act effectively or act too late to prevent catastrophe, the climate camp movement has emerged. In Britain, activists have occupied land to build protest camps in opposition to coal-fired power stations at Drax in Yorkshire, Kingsnorth in Kent, Heathrow airport and the City of London, Britain's financial heart. This climate camp movement is spreading worldwide with camps in Australia, Belgium, Ecuador and the US. Radical greens from all over the world have played a major part in protests at IMF summits, WTO meetings and similar global gatherings.

Individuals can, of course, build community groups to further green politics without being involved in either direct action or elections. In the first decade of the 21st century the concept of Transition Towns has grown, based on the idea that communities should plan for a future in which they can live sustainably without relying on fossil fuels. This movement – originally created in Kinsale, Ireland – is growing fast and is fostering a sense of community in the present even as it works towards a sustainable future.

Green politics also includes, to some extent, the contribution of environmental NGOs, the more radical of which sometimes put forward all the key elements of a green political agenda. However conservation groups that just emphasize environmental reformism are difficult to categorize as fully green in the political sense. Of course boundaries are often blurred and it would not really be in the spirit of green politics to exclude some networks or NGOs with a cry of 'Ungreen! Ungreen!'

Green politics is, to repeat, not just about political parties but includes wider social movements. In turn, the philosophies that underpin green politics extend beyond environmental concern. Green politics is more than environmentalism but increasing evidence of climate change and other eco threats has fueled its growth. The next chapter explores the ecological crisis in more detail.

1 www.global.greens.org.au/charter/UTGnewethic.html **2** Peter Gould, *Early Green Politics*, Harvester Press, 1988. **3** Derek Wall, *Green History*, Routledge, 1993. **4** http://tinyurl.com/yj7e3uv **5** http://tinyurl.com/yf3hqbw **6** www.globalgreens.org/alert/saruul_agvaandorj

2 The overheating earth

Almost all other problems faced by humanity are dwarfed by the specter of climate change, yet mainstream politicians seem incapable of rising to the challenge. Green campaigners are alone in challenging the world's addiction to economic growth but can point to the positive example of an unlikely convert to their way of thinking – Cuba...

WHILE GREEN POLITICS is about more than the environment, an unfolding environmental crisis is the main inspiration behind the growth and development of green politics in recent years. Environmental problems are not new – anti-pollution laws were introduced in medieval London – but what is new is their global scale. Climate change is increasingly likely to have devastating effects globally. However, climate change is just the most visible manifestation of a wider ecological crisis, which threatens humanity and the rest of nature.

The principle behind climate change is simple. Carbon dioxide (CO_2) and other greenhouse gases such as methane create a layer of molecules in the atmosphere that trap heat like a pane of glass in a greenhouse. The burning of fossil fuels – coal, oil and natural gas – over the last 200 years has released ever larger amounts of CO_2 into the atmosphere. Other climate-change-inducing gases such as nitrous oxide (emitted by jet aircraft) and methane (much of it from cattle raised for the meat industry) have also increased in the atmosphere. Although climate change is a complex topic, and other factors influence temperatures, increasing levels of greenhouse gases in the atmosphere are already leading to rising temperatures.

If all known coal deposits were burned the Earth would become too hot for human existence. Yet we are burning such deposits of coal, oil and natural gas – locked into geological strata over millions of years – almost as soon as we find them.

The consequences of climate change are disturbing. Rising temperatures will lead to rising sea levels, which will potentially flood huge areas. While wealthier countries can build sea defenses, poorer regions of the world – particularly small islands – are likely to be swamped. Nicholas Stern's report on climate change for the UK government argued that the economic and human costs of climate change are likely to be massive.

Stern considers that 'an overwhelming body of scientific evidence now clearly indicates that climate change is a serious and urgent issue'.[1] This evidence suggests that if annual greenhouse gas emissions continue to grow at current levels, global temperatures will rise by between 3 and 10 degrees Celsius by 2100. The consequences are startling.

A four-degree rise in temperatures would mean entire regions of the world would be too hot to grow agricultural crops. Australia would be among the countries hit hardest. Glaciers that provide water for hundreds of millions of people are already disappearing. The report attributed rises in food prices during 2008 in part to climate change and crops are already failing in some parts of world due to climatic disruption. Most of the world's rice is grown less than one meter above sea level.

According to Stern, 22 of the world's 50 largest cities are at risk from coastal surges. 'The world's major financial centers (London, New York and Tokyo) are all located in coastal areas,' the report points out. 'The insurance industry estimates that, in London alone, at least $220 billion of assets lie on the floodplain.' Some 200 million people live on coastal floodplains that are less than one meter above sea level.

The concentration of greenhouse gases in the

A world without ice?

This warming is irreversible on the human scale. Even if the atmospheric concentrations of greenhouse gases were stabilized immediately, global warming would make its effects felt for nearly a thousand years, because the temperature of enormous masses of ocean water takes a very long time to homogenize. In the absence of any stabilization, the mechanism would inevitably speed up dramatically and would unleash extremely dangerous phenomena such as the disintegration of the polar icecaps or the release of the enormous quantities of methane contained in frozen ground (permafrost), indeed even in the depths of the oceans.

It would be erroneous and dangerous to gamble on the idea that the exhaustion of the stocks of coal, oil and gas will happen in time to protect humanity from these major risks. In fact, proven fossil-fuel reserves (in particular of coal) are amply sufficient to cause an uncontrollable acceleration. In this event, the Earth would be likely to rediscover conditions that it has not known for 65 million years and that humanity has consequently never experienced: a world without ice, where the level of the seas would be about a hundred meters higher than the present level. ∎

Daniel Tanuro, International Viewpoint
www.internationalviewpoint.org/spip.php?article164

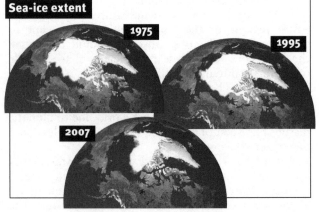

Sea-ice extent

1975

1995

2007

atmosphere has risen from 220 parts per million (ppm) in the 19th century to 430ppm today. Stern argues that, while adaptation is possible through sea defenses, unless further growth is limited to keep atmospheric concentrations to a maximum of 550ppm

– which would require a 70-per-cent cut in emissions – feedback mechanisms such as the thawing of permafrost will lead to disaster. A more recent study by the Tyndall Centre for Climate Change Research finds even Stern's gloomy picture too optimistic.

The feedback mechanisms that so concern Stern are worrying. One of the most scary is methane release from the world's permafrost. This permanently frozen marshland, found mainly in Canada and Siberia, is beginning to melt as a result of the rising global temperatures. As the permafrost melts, it releases methane that has hitherto been locked up. Methane is 23 times more powerful as a greenhouse gas than carbon dioxide so the release of these deposits will increase temperatures further, melting more permafrost and thereby releasing more methane in an extremely vicious circle.

There are many more such feedback mechanisms. For example, as glaciers melt, white surfaces that reflect heat and thereby reduce global warming are eroded. As darker surfaces such as rock are revealed, climate change will accelerate and more icy surfaces will melt.

Climate change degrades ecosystems and often makes them less effective at absorbing CO_2. Entire species are likely to become extinct and ecosystems destabilized. Rainforests may disappear and deserts may spread. Forests have acted as carbon sinks absorbing excess CO_2 but with environmental degradation this could be reversed.

The increase in CO_2 will not only increase temperatures but is leading to the acidification of the world's oceans. The seas of our planet are slightly alkaline and home to shellfish, plankton and other species with calcium carbonate structures. CO_2 is being absorbed by the seas which within a few decades will become acidic and this will kill the species with calcium carbonate shells. The consequences, almost forgotten by the world's politicians and media, will be to wreck ecosystems and destroy fisheries. The results are difficult to think about calmly.

Other eco problems

Climate change is part of a much wider network of closely linked ecological problems. In addition to acidification from CO_2, a series of other problems is degrading the world's oceans. Pollution is leading to extinction. Plastic and other rubbish is collecting in huge islands. Overfishing has led to recent reports suggesting that all commercial fish stocks will be gone by 2050.

Coral reefs are important to marine ecosystems and provide breeding grounds for fish and many other species. However, the corals are being progressively bleached out of existence. Coral is very sensitive to small rises in temperature, which cause its photosynthetic symbionts to become more light sensitive and die. If the bleaching is severe, the coral may find it impossible to recover. Corals also absorb CO_2 so their destruction in turn makes climate change more likely. The oceans have risen in temperature by one degree Celsius over the last century. This sounds like a tiny increase but it has already produced severe bleaching. Even the more modest likely projections for temperature increases of two degrees Celsius over the next few decades could destroy coral globally, with appalling consequences for marine life.

Mangrove swamps are also under attack, often drained to build shrimp pools or built over for development projects such as hotels. One of the reasons why the 2004 tsunami, a tidal wave caused by an undersea earthquake, was so devastating to Indonesia, Thailand and other countries was because of the removal of mangrove swamps, which would otherwise have diffused the force of the killer wave. Half the planet's mangrove swamps have been destroyed in the last 30 years. Your shrimp curry metaphorically contains human blood.

Rainforests continue to be assaulted in many parts of the world, cut down to make space for cattle or logged for timber. As oil prices have risen, there has been more pressure to extract oil from ecologically vital areas, including rainforests. Rainforests are often replaced by monocultures of eucalyptus or other crops, which can be exploited for cash.

To some extent countries like the US and UK have exported pollution by exporting production to countries like India and China. The once-filthy Thames may be clean but the Yangtze is now taking the strain from industrial production.

Ultimately, what goes around comes around – we live in a highly globalized world. Communications, culture and economics are increasingly global, with both positive and negative results, and so too are environmental problems. An insult to one is increasingly an insult to all. Climate change is the best illustration of this, but there are many other symptoms of the multi-faceted global environmental crisis. One of these may be that human fertility, particularly

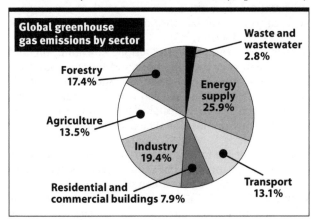

Global greenhouse gas emissions by sector

Waste and wastewater 2.8%
Forestry 17.4%
Energy supply 25.9%
Agriculture 13.5%
Industry 19.4%
Transport 13.1%
Residential and commercial buildings 7.9%

male fertility, is falling sharply in many parts of the world. While scientists blame a number of factors, including smoking, alcohol and junk food, pollution is a factor, according to Sajal Dutta, president of the Bengal chapter of the Federation of Obstetric and Gynaecological Societies of India: 'The fact that a large number of men are unable to impregnate women is because of poor quality sperm or low sperm count. Excessive chlorine and arsenic in potable water, smoking and breathing in air that is as bad as smoking 40 cigarettes a day affect sperm quality.'[2]

An anti-pollution activist in China argues: 'The government is focused on economic growth, so, more often than not, they think less about the environment. All they will do is urge companies to reduce levels of pollution. They won't shut them down.'[3] The observation could just as easily have been made by an anti-pollution activist in any capitalist country.

China is making some modest progress to clean its economy, despite decades in which little has been done to combat pollution, with highly polluting industrial plants often placed near rivers and densely populated areas. Technological advances and regulation may drastically reduce the emissions per plant but, even if such gains materialize, they are likely to be wiped out by extra production.

Increasing rates of production, consumption and waste mean that there is more and more demand for fossil fuels, metals and minerals. Such demand fuels the destruction of forests and other valuable habitats to gain such resources. Such destruction leads to yet more pressure on the global environment – yet another vicious circle.

Biodiversity is falling as more and more species are faced with extinction. Pollution directly kills human beings – in a sense, environmental catastrophe has been with us for decades already. Pollutants injure millions of people in poorer parts of the world, whether in

Mexico City, where smog is a killer, or as a result of the proliferating environmental problems in China. Yet even in Britain, where air quality is somewhat better, partly because most of its manufactured goods are now produced in other parts of the world, around 35,000 people a year may die because of poor air quality. Microscopic particles from car exhausts are the main cause.[4]

Run-off from nitrogen fertilizers is another major but often forgotten form of pollution. Large areas of the Gulf of Mexico are dead zones because fertilizer run-off from agribusiness in the US has removed oxygen, killing sea life. In 2009, meanwhile, fertilizers led to a huge increase in seaweed growth that washed on to beaches in Brittany, France, and then rotted, emitting a poisonous gas which killed horses and threatened human health.

Economic growth is the root of the problem

This multi-faceted environmental crisis has economic roots. Greens certainly believe that there needs to be tighter regulation aimed at preventing and cleaning up the various ecological problems, but see ever-increasing economic growth as the root cause. While technology may allow us to produce goods in cleaner ways, there is a contradiction at the heart of the pursuit of growth. The more we consume and produce in the supposed pursuit of a better life, the greater is the inevitable increase in pollution and waste. Many environmentalists point to the Jevons Paradox. William Stanley Jevons, a 19th-century economist, argued in his book *The Coal Question* that technological improvements tend to increase the use of resources. The paradox also applies to greener forms of technology. An excellent example is car use. 'Green' cars tend to increase pollution because any efficiency gains are outstripped by the growth in the number of cars. If cars become, say, 10-per-cent more fuel efficient, but the number of cars on the roads

Top 10 carbon-emitting countries

The top 10 carbon-emitting countries, with reader countries not in the top 10 listed below with their global position. Note that Australia's per capita emissions are higher even than those of the US. The places with the highest carbon emissions per person are, however, small dependencies or countries such as Gibraltar, the US Virgin Islands and Qatar.

Country	Amount emitted 2007 (million of tonnes CO_2 equivalent)	
1 China	6284	(5 tonnes per person)
2 United States	6007	(20 tonnes per person)
3 Russia	1673	(12 tonnes per person)
4 India	1401	(1 tonne per person)
5 Japan	1262	(10 tonnes per person)
6 Germany	853	(10 tonnes per person)
7 Canada	590	(18 tonnes per person)
8 United Kingdom	564	(9 tonnes per person)
9 South Korea	516	(11 tonnes per person)
10 Iran	490	(7 tonnes per person)
12 Australia	456	(22 tonnes per person)
63 Ireland	45	(11 tonnes per person)
69 New Zealand/Aotearoa	39	(9 tonnes per person)

Source: US Energy Information Administration

grows by 20 per cent, more fuel will be used. We need more radical alternatives because relentless increases in economic growth, even if accompanied by cleaner, greener ways of doing things, still tend to damage the environment.

Green activists and politicians tend to be the only ones prepared to confront the issue of economic growth, as when 2008 Green Party US presidential candidate Cynthia McKinney grasped the nettle by campaigning on the slogan 'Keep the Oil in the Soil'. In contrast, most conventional solutions to environmental problems avoid the question of growth – as do all the mainstream political parties. The present global framework for climate change, for example, is based upon a complex system of carbon trading which is often criticized by green campaigners as, at best ineffective, and at worst likely to increase the pressure on fragile ecosystems.

Carbon trading turns the atmosphere into a commodity which can be bought or sold. In place of regulation to prevent climate change, it offers a market in which countries buy and sell the right to pollute. This is the basis of the Kyoto Protocol, which, ironically, was originally a product of US corporate lobbying – despite President George W Bush's subsequent steadfast rejection of it. Many environmentalists are reluctant to point out the problems associated with Kyoto, thankful for crumbs of climate-change comfort.

Carbon emissions are hard to measure and policing such a market is difficult. Depressingly, they mean that the well-off can buy the right to pollute by using dubious offsetting schemes. In the UK, for example, although on paper there are very strict targets for reducing CO_2, emissions exceeding those targets can be offset. This means that, if the UK government fails to cut its carbon emissions sufficiently, it can pretend it has done the trick by paying other countries to make carbon cuts. In the European Union, companies have been given CO_2 permits that have actually allowed them to produce more emissions than they had previously. Moreover, campaigners like the Durban Group for Climate Justice in South Africa have noted that emissions trading is sometimes used to fund projects that may be environmentally damaging.

'The problems with carbon trading are compounded when carbon credits are used to fund destructive projects like large dams and industrial tree plantations, which is a frequent occurrence in the Global South,' argues Cristian Guerrero, a climate justice organizer based in Mexico. 'This never benefits the local populations who become displaced,' he says, 'and it harms biodiversity too.'[5]

Similarly, in a letter to former UN Secretary-

The overheating earth

General Kofi Annan, Soumitra Ghosh of the National Forum of Forest Peoples and Forest Workers in India notes: 'We're creating a sort of "climate apartheid", wherein the poorest and darkest-skinned pay the highest price – with their health, their land, and, in some cases, with their lives – for continued carbon profligacy by the rich.'

Such carbon trading is unfair, then – richer parts of the world can go on polluting and pay for others who are poorer to reduce their carbon output. More fundamentally, many greens argue that carbon trading allows for both outright fraud and dubious forms of

Carbon cop-outs

From the World Cup to HSBC and BP's offset petrol, individuals, organizations and corporations have been keen to prove their climate-friendly credentials by going 'carbon neutral'. The success of the different schemes reflects the fact that there is an increase in popular awareness about the need to engage with climate change. But are these schemes offering a valid approach to the problem, or are they detracting from the real action that needs to take place?...

Some environmentalists were dubious about both the ethics and the efficacy of carbon offsets from the beginning, but the dark clouds of doubt and controversy gathered throughout 2006. In April, articles appeared in the [British] press suggesting that some 40 per cent of the mango trees in southern India that Coldplay had sponsored to offset the emissions from the recording of their second album had died. The villagers who were supposed to be the benefactors of the scheme made allegations of unfulfilled promises and project mismanagement, and there was a breakdown in relations between the Carbon Neutral Company and its project partner in India. Yet, for months afterwards, fans of the band were still being sold dedicated trees in the plantations that were still being portrayed as a glowing success story.

In October, the UK Advertising Standards Authority (ASA) ordered the Scottish and Southern Energy Group (SSE) to stop making claims about 'neutralizing' its customers' emissions in its leaflets. In the contentious advert, the SSE claimed to 'plant trees to balance out the CO_2 that your gas heating and household waste produces'. Although the SSE was able to provide figures on what emissions the average household produced, the lack of scientific knowledge about the carbon cycle meant that it was unable to provide sufficient evidence that the number of trees it planted would match or exceed the level accounting that mean that fossil fuel use is likely to accelerate.

Commenting on carbon trading payments made to an Indian fertilizer company – GFL – associated with severe pollution, Kevin Smith from Carbon Trade Watch noted: 'The carbon market is riddled with projects like GFL. It's not like this project is the bad apple – the whole barrel is rotten. Time and again we're seeing evidence of gross injustices being carried out – people being evicted to make way for dams and waste incinerators being built in residential areas. Carbon trading has been the subject of a very slick PR

---

of emissions, and it was thus in breach of the ASA guidelines. It has yet to be seen what impact this ruling will have on the countless other spurious 'neutralizing' claims made by similar offset schemes.

These incidents, and many others, have highlighted some of the technical problems with offset schemes, and have brought the environmental or social shortcomings of specific projects into focus. Less has been written about how offset schemes are fundamentally ineffective in addressing climate change through their emphasis on personal consumption, lifestyle and individual action...

The act of commodification at the heart of offset schemes assigns a financial value to the impetus that someone may feel to take climate action, and neatly transforms this potential to bring about change into another market transaction. There is then no urgent need for people to question the underlying assumptions about the nature of the social and economic structures that brought about climate change in the first place. One just has to click and pay the assigned price to get 'experts' to take action on your behalf. Not only is it ineffective and based on half-baked guessing games and dubious science, it is also very disempowering for the participants.

The single most effective – and incontrovertible – way of dealing with climate change is drastically to limit the quantity of fossil fuels being extracted. Providing support for communities who are resisting the efforts of the industries to extract and burn ever-increasing quantities, therefore, is one of the most important strategies in dealing with climate change. Yet it is the least encouraged because, unlike carbon offsets, it involves posing a critical challenge to the established systems of corporate power and societal organization.

Kevin Smith, *Red Pepper*, www.redpepper.org.uk/Carbon-cop-outs

campaign portraying it as the answer to climate change, so investigations such as this are very important.'[6]

Given that a questioning of economic growth is off limits, and any solutions to the problem of climate change need to allow for business as usual, there is predictable enthusiasm for technological fixes. One such example is carbon capture, where the idea is that new coal power plants should be built in the hope that CO_2 might be captured and stored underground. The more logical alternative of investing in renewable energy is less attractive to business interests and remains underdeveloped.

Nuclear power is also seen as an answer to the energy problem, despite the fact that, from nuclear waste dumping to the potential for nuclear weapons proliferation, it involves huge dangers – and the carbon footprint of the uranium mining industry on which nuclear energy depends is not discussed. In turn, incinerators producing microscopic particles that are injurious to human health are promoted as a solution to the waste problem. Neither incinerators nor nuclear power can be seen as serious green alternatives.

Meanwhile, the great car economy drives on into the future. Instead of working to make public transport so efficient and extensive that cars become less attractive, corporations and governments have turned to biofuels as a way of keeping the world's car fleet on the roads. Biofuels are largely based on energy crops such as palm oil. Bizarrely, to fuel cars in a supposedly 'green' way, rainforests in Latin America, Africa and Southeast Asia are being cut down and replaced by palm oil plantations. Cutting the forest to make way for biofuel plantations is represented as a means of reducing CO_2 emissions when actually it increases them sharply. It destroys wildlife too – in Indonesia and Malaysia, biofuels are the biggest threat to orangutans. Biofuels are also associated with human rights abuse, especially in Colombia, which is the main source of the European Union's palm oil.

A better way

To deal with climate change, we need to move towards a zero carbon economy and do our utmost to preserve carbon sinks such as the rainforest. Technology will play a role, but not in pursuit of illusory technofixes. Instead, campaigners across the world have argued for a Green New Deal, which would involve massive investment in renewable energy.

Renewable energy sources are very diverse, from wind to solar, from geothermal to tidal. During the European elections of 2009, Greens in the UK campaigned on buses fueled by used cooking fat. So while Greens are critical of growing crops for fuel, which can damage the environment and push up food prices, they are far from unwilling to use waste as a potential fuel.

Green politics is about changing the structures, so that individuals can more easily reduce their consumption of carbon. Affordable and effective public transport and cycling facilities form part of the solution, while Green policies of economic localization also have the potential to reduce energy use without making life harder for us as individuals. If local shops and services are available, this will cut down the need to make journeys – and if the products in those shops are sourced more locally as well, the carbon emissions associated with their freight will also be reduced.

Many greens support the idea of contraction and convergence. This is the notion that each human being on the planet should be limited to using a certain amount of CO_2 equivalent and that these 'quotas' should gradually converge, so that people in rich and poor countries ultimately bear the same burden. Simply allowing the rich to buy the right to emit more, which is essentially what happens at present, would no longer

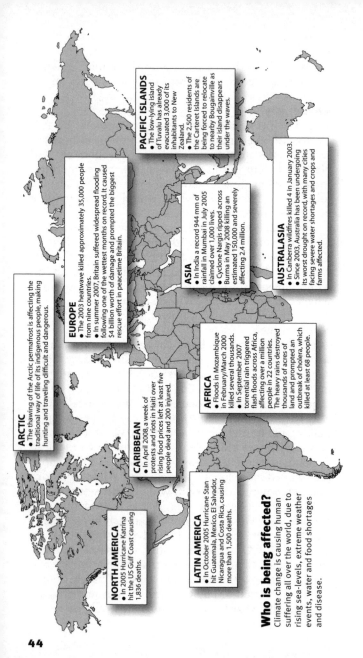

ARCTIC
• The thawing of the Arctic permafrost is affecting the traditional way of life of its indigenous people, making hunting and traveling difficult and dangerous.

EUROPE
• The 2003 heatwave killed approximately 35,000 people from nine countries.
• In summer 2007, Britain suffered widespread flooding following one of the wettest months on record. It caused $4 billion worth of damage and prompted the biggest rescue effort in peacetime Britain.

PACIFIC ISLANDS
• The low-lying island of Tuvalu has already evacuated 3,000 of its inhabitants to New Zealand.
• The 2,500 residents of the Carteret Islands are being forced to relocate to nearby Bougainville as their island disappears under the waves.

ASIA
• In India a record 944 mm of rainfall in Mumbai in July 2005 claimed over 1,000 lives.
• Cyclone Nargis ripped across Burma in May 2008 killing an estimated 150,000 and severely affecting 2.4 million.

AUSTRALASIA
• In Canberra wildfires killed 4 in January 2003.
• Since 2003, Australia has been undergoing its worst drought on record, with many cities facing severe water shortages and crops and farms affected.

NORTH AMERICA
• In 2005 Hurricane Katrina hit the US Gulf Coast causing 1,836 deaths.

CARIBBEAN
• In April 2008, a week of protests and riots in Haiti over rising food prices left at least five people dead and 200 injured.

AFRICA
• Floods in Mozambique in February/March 2000 killed several thousands.
• In September 2007 torrential rain triggered flash floods across Africa, affecting over a million people in 22 countries. The heavy rains destroyed thousands of acres of land and prompted an outbreak of cholera, which killed at least 68 people.

LATIN AMERICA
• In October 2005 Hurricane Stan hit Guatemala, Mexico, El Salvador, Nicaragua and Costa Rica, causing more than 1,500 deaths.

Who is being affected?

Climate change is causing human suffering all over the world, due to rising sea-levels, extreme weather events, water and food shortages and disease.

44

be allowed. The high consumption and high waste of the wealthiest countries is clearly unsustainable – on average, US citizens produce 20 times the carbon emissions of the rest of the planet's population.[7]

There is at present one country in the world that has achieved a form of sustainable development, having reduced ecological impact while raising living standards. It has not used carbon trading to achieve this success and its example does not generate income for bankers, so its achievement has been ignored by policymakers.

The country is Cuba. It has succeeded in significantly cutting its carbon emissions per capita by reducing its reliance on fossil fuels. Cuba has not always been a green example. For many decades it did not even have a minister of the environment. However, after the collapse of the Soviet Union in 1990, it stopped receiving cheap oil from what is now Russia. Faced with energy shortages, it was forced into introducing a crash green energy program.

Cuba has worked hard to generate energy through renewables. Schools in rural areas, for example, derive their energy from solar panels. Recently, a wind map has been produced for the whole island and wind turbines are springing up.

Perhaps the most important part of Cuba's green revolution is agricultural. It has turned to organic farming in a major way, which does not require oil-derived inputs. Permaculture, a special form of organic farming originally developed by the Australian writer Bill Mollison, was introduced in Cuba during the 1990s. This uses ecological principles to minimize energy and labor inputs and to maximize output. The method uses tree crops and mulches to avoid the need for labor-intensive digging. Another principle of permaculture is companion planting, where inter-cropping of different plants is used to reduce pests and increase fertility. Composting is vital. Worm bins are used to turn waste into natural fertilizers and mulches.

The overheating earth

Talk to almost anyone who visited Havana in the 1990s and they'll say the city exploded with gardeners. Today, rooftops and the smallest scraps of land are used to grow food. It quite literally stopped people from starving and Havana is virtually self-sufficient in fresh fruit and vegetables. So rather than low-carbon solutions leading to a lower standard of living, permaculture has actually increased prosperity for Cubans.

The Cuban experience is instructive, yet at present climate solutions are in the hands of world's bankers rather than scientists or even permaculturists. The key changes we need to protect global ecology demand the implementation of major structural change to make a low carbon (even zero carbon) future possible, desirable and practical. It's quite simple when you think about it: tackling climate change means huge cuts in our carbon emissions and protecting the environment by promoting ecological practices. Snared by a system of carbon trading that patently does not work, the world is failing to take serious action. Putting our trust in carbon trading is like coping with the threat of lung cancer by lighting up another cigarette and hoping you can encourage someone else to give up if you give them a cash incentive controlled by a hedge fund.

While awareness of climate change and other major environmental problems has certainly heightened over the last two decades, effective and concerted action to promote solutions still seems a distant prospect and time is running out. Environmental concern has to translate into green political action within a matter of months and years rather than decades if we are to have a viable and comfortable future.

1 Nicholas Stern, *The economics of climate change: the Stern review*, UK Treasury, London 2007. 2 http://tinyurl.com/y9m3l5x 3 http://tinyurl.com/yhskb5b 4 'Air pollution may cause 35,000 premature deaths a year in Britain', *The Guardian*, 23 Feb 2010. 5 Cited in Derek Wall, 'Costing the Earth', *Red Pepper*, Dec 2006. 6 http://tinyurl.com/l74m4q 7 http://tinyurl.com/lqlrsx

3 Green philosophy

Greens tend to share a core philosophy that sees humans' relationship with the rest of nature as central. The political principles that emerge from this are, however, surprisingly diverse – from ecofeminism to ecoanarchism, ecosocialism to ecofascism.

GREEN POLITICS IS underpinned by a distinct philosophy based on a series of linked ethical concerns that are often ignored or forgotten by other ideologies, including liberalism and conservatism. Perhaps the most important element of green philosophy is an 'ecocentric' approach. While other political ideologies have generally viewed nature as a quarry – something to be dug up and exploited for short-term gain – greens put the environment at the center of their concerns. The 'ecocentric' element of green philosophy stresses that other species – and even the Earth itself – have moral standing; they cannot just be used without regard, merely as instruments to benefit humanity. This means that even if the severe environmental problems discussed in the previous chapter did not threaten human society, greens would still seek to combat them, because they would threaten the diversity and beauty of our planet. In essence, greens argue that the rest of nature has ethical status and cannot be used for human gain without thought.

The phrase 'deep ecology', coined by the Norwegian writer Arne Naess in 1973, is often used instead of the term 'deep green' or 'ecocentric'. His first principle of deep ecology concisely sums up the approach outlined above: 'The well-being and flourishing of human and nonhuman life on Earth have value in themselves. These values are independent of the usefulness of the nonhuman world for human purposes'.[1]

An ecocentric approach draws on the science of ecology to show that we are closely linked to other species. Life is a web and human beings are just as much a part of the web as goats or ryegrass. To pretend that humanity is separate from the rest of creation is a form of madness from an ecocentric point of view.

Green political philosophy clearly includes an element of animal rights. While notions of rights can be difficult to define with absolute precision, animals have moral status for greens and Green parties have campaigned against vivisection, factory farming, bullfighting and other forms of cruelty. However, deep ecology moves beyond animal rights to include whole ecosystems. This throws up some very difficult intellectual dilemmas. Can plants or mountains have rights? How do we define 'harm',

---

The eight principles of deep ecology

1 The well-being and flourishing of human and non-human life on Earth have value in themselves. These values are independent of the usefulness of the non-human world for human purposes.

2 Richness and diversity of life-forms contribute to the realization of these values and are also values in themselves.

3 Humans have no right to reduce this richness and diversity except to satisfy vital needs.

4 The flourishing of human life and cultures is compatible with a substantial decrease of the human population. The flourishing of non-human life requires such a decrease.

5 Present human interference with the non-human world is excessive, and the situation is rapidly worsening.

6 Policies must therefore be changed. The changes in policies affect basic economic, technological, and ideological structures. The resulting state of affairs will be deeply different from the present.

7 The ideological change is mainly that of appreciating quality (dwelling in situations of inherent worth) rather than adhering to an increasingly higher standard of living. There will be a profound awareness of the difference between big and great.

8 Those who subscribe to the foregoing points have an obligation directly or indirectly to participate in the attempt to implement the necessary changes.

Arne Naess and George Sessions, revised 21 January 2000
www.all-creatures.org/articles/env-theeight.html

---

given that many species prey upon each other and perhaps all have their own species-centric views? If squirrels were the dominant species on the planet, gifted with intelligence, they might spend their time exterminating cats and genetically engineering better-tasting walnuts. Nonetheless Naess's first principle of deep ecology is clear and has numerous consequences for green politics.

'Rights' are also extended to future generations, with greens trying to be good ancestors to our children and our children's children, as we noted in Chapter 1. Inter-generational equity is the idea that we should leave things in at least as a good state as we found them. One of the earliest formulations of this idea comes, perhaps surprisingly, from Karl Marx, who stated:

> 'Even an entire society, a nation, or all simultaneously existing societies taken together, are not the owners of the earth. They are simply its possessors, its beneficiaries, and have to bequeath it in an improved state to succeeding generations as *boni patres familias* [good heads of the household].'[2]

The Nobel Prize-winning political scientist and economist Elinor Ostrom is even more ambitious and talks of the need for a 'seven-generation rule'. She argues that when planning major projects we should consider the effect on the next seven generations.[3]

This concern with being good ancestors and respecting the needs of future generations, like the deep ecology ethic itself, throws up some difficult questions. For example, what do we mean by improvement? Greens would stress ecological sustainability, while others might argue for financial investment and economic expansion. Despite Marx's words, the Left has often forgotten the need to respect future generations but greens believe that the human beings of the future deserve consideration, as well as nature. The citizens to come should be given more weight when we decide what practical policies to adopt in the here and now. Ecological problems and the exhaustion of scarce and vital resources need to be tackled from a green political point of view if we are to bequeath a future to our children and grandchildren.

Knowing our limits

Green philosophy also contains the notion of 'limits'. Infinite economic growth on a finite planet is seen as unsustainable. If we go on producing, consuming and wasting at ever-increasing rates, this is likely to be extremely damaging not just to future generations but to the rest of nature and humanity today. From climate change to peak oil, the impossibility of ever-greater economic growth is another fundamental principle that makes green politics radically different from other ideologies. This notion of limits fits with the ecocentric principle: even if unlimited economic growth were possible, it would not be desirable for greens because of its impact on the rest of nature.

Ecocentrism puts limits on humanity. Marx called for respect for nature, while the founding father of liberalism, John Stuart Mill, advocated a green philosophy of limits, believing that zero economic growth might be combined with greater equality to create a better society. However, both liberals and the Left have generally advocated limitless economic expansion, along with the supporters of other non-green ideologies.

More radically, some greens, though not all, have sought to limit human population growth as well as economic expansion. This approach has been attacked for being potentially authoritarian and for distracting attention from the environmental damage done by economic expansion and the misuse of technology. The economist Amartya Sen has been particularly critical of those who focus on the population of the world's poor rather than the over-consumption of those with the most wealth.

'It remains true that one additional American typically has a larger negative impact on the ozone layer, global warmth and other elements of the earth's environment than dozens of Indians and Zimbabweans put together. Those who argue for the immediate need for forceful population control in the Third World to preserve the global environment must first recognize this elementary fact.'[4]

Green politics is also holistic. Holism is the idea that by dividing things into parts we learn less and less about their true nature. We live in a reductionist society, where academic and other disciplines are increasingly specialized. Greens, in contrast, suggest that, to understand something, we need to see it as part of a wider system. Ecology is a holistic science, based on understanding the relationship of diverse species. An ecocentric attitude that sees human beings as a part of nature and the idea of limits comes from this holistic viewpoint.

Many greens have seen a reductionist attitude to science as a source of environmental and other ills. Newtonian physics and Descartes' approach of reductionist reason have been seen as sources of a philosophy that uses nature in an instrumental way and ultimately degrades human beings as well. The physicist Fritjof Capra and the philosopher Charlene Spretnak in their book *Green Politics* argue that changing scientific viewpoints, particularly derived from quantum physics, provide the potential for a holistic philosophy. They see such holism as the basis of green ideas and politics.

'Visionary/holistic greens have as their central concern and guiding principle the evolution of a new society based on ways of thinking and being that reflect the interconnected nature of all phenomena. They want people to move beyond the mechanistic world view that has dominated Western thinking for the past 300 years to a fuller understanding of the subtle relationships and dynamic flux that comprise life on Earth.'[5]

Holism may appear esoteric, and its tangled roots in science, Eastern religion, Hegelian philosophy and the musing of poets such as William Blake seems a little remote from practical politics. Nonetheless, there are practical implications of a holistic political philosophy. For example, environmental problems must be seen ecologically as a product of diverse causes. Simple solutions usually turn out to be too simplistic. Holism should not be seen as a form of new age mysticism but as an emphasis on network connections. A holistic approach, which seeks to look at problems in a context of diverse connections, can lead to more effective solutions.

For example, climate change is a product of particular economic forces and attitudes, so simply introducing more renewable energy may not get to the root of the problem. In a society where growth is so important, if the expansion of renewable energy is not accompanied by reduced fossil-fuel use, climate change will remain a problem. Demands for more resources that lead to the destruction of key ecosystems will fuel climate change, even if we use fewer fossil fuels. Green politics looks at prevention and structural solutions because of this holistic ecological approach.

All areas of policy can be treated holistically. A good example is healthcare. Reductionist approaches see illness as the product of clear causes that can be treated with medicines and other forms of technology. While greens do not reject technological solutions, they stress that ill-health is a product of environment and social causes and that prevention is always better than cure. Mental health problems, rather than being simply caused by a faulty gene, are often a product of depression brought about through poverty or alienation. A more equal society is likely to be a much healthier one. There is greater awareness of preventative medicine based on a healthier environment and society – and recent restrictions on tobacco smoking have helped foster this preventative climate. On the other hand, pharmaceutical companies are often keen to medicalize social problems in the interests of selling expensive drug treatments.

Permaculture, the practice invented by the Australian Bill Mollison and mentioned in the last chapter in the context of Cuba, is a good example of a holistic approach. Rather than pests being blasted with poisons, they are discouraged through companion planting. Rather than using artificial fertilizers that wash into rivers and cause pollution, organic waste is recycled as compost. Permaculture looks at food production within a wider ecological context; it could be said to be simply a modern term for traditional practices followed by indigenous peoples who both dwell in and protect the rainforest. Green politics is like the application to the wider society and economy of permacultural principles in agriculture.

Science and solutions

Green politics has a complex relationship with science. The effects of nuclear power, acid rain, climate change and threats to biodiversity: these are all problems that have been identified and explained by scientific research. Scientific issues and problems are vital to the green movement. It was the science in such reports as *Limits to Growth* that fostered the creation of Green parties in the first place. However, science does not always provide automatic solutions to problems such as climate change or deforestation. Indeed, greens believe that the application of science via technological solutions can lead to disastrous consequences unless great care is taken. The very complexity of ecological systems makes it difficult to predict with any certainty the effects of particular measures or policies. Unintended results can often occur, and a certain caution is appropriate when applying scientific solutions to complex ecological problems. While such uncertainty should not justify doing nothing in the face of severe environmental problems such as climate change, it does suggest that quick-fix technical solutions may create nasty side-effects and should be undertaken with extreme care. Greens tend to be very suspicious of big geo-engineering projects that purport to address ecological problems, as with the idea of scattering reflective particles into the atmosphere to combat global warming.

Greens are also critical of technological solutions because they believe that technology has to be seen in a social context. Often social problems such as poverty are dealt with using technical means that avoid examining underlying causes. The Green Revolution of the 1970s is a good example. This used new hybrid plants to increase crop yields in India and other developing countries; it was assumed that this would be an effective solution to hunger and poverty in poorer parts of the world. However, though it succeeded in raising agricultural yields, it also strengthened the position of large landowners at the expense of the poor, thus leading to greater inequality. As the Indian activist and scientist Vandana Shiva has noted, the Green Revolution also led to severe ecological ill-effects. Boosting food production in the short term has therefore led to a series of environmental problems such as loss of biodiversity and soil erosion that may destroy future productivity.

Critics argue that greens cherry-pick from science, using it to justify their concerns in some areas such as climate change but ignoring it when it challenges their beliefs. Greens respond that failure to place technology within a wider context – socially and morally, as well as ecologically – often leads to disaster and unforeseen consequences. The magic bullet kills more often than it cures.

Naturalism

Green philosophy can appear to be naturalistic. Naturalism is the idea that, as human society is part of nature, laws of nature can be discovered and used to shape human conduct. What could be greener than the notion that human beings should obey the laws of nature? The problem, though, is that nature works in different ways in different areas of the natural world. The behavior of microbes, for example, tells us little about the sexual habits of bears, let alone the political choices that human beings have to make.

The green anarchist Murray Bookchin condemned deep ecologists for being naturalistic and argued that in particular they ignored the social causes of environmental problems. Bookchin argued that human societies cannot be reduced to biology; we can only solve ecological problems by rejecting naturalism and deep ecology. He reacted angrily to extreme statements from US deep ecologists such as Dave Foreman, who went so far as to say that they welcomed the AIDS pandemic and famines in Africa because they reduced the human population and therefore the damage to nature. Notwithstanding the reactionary views of some, deep ecologists should not all be tarred with the same brush. Arne Naess, the writer, mountaineer and Second World War resistance fighter who coined the term deep ecology, called in his famous essay on the topic[6] for exactly the kind of social and democratic values that Bookchin believed in.

Using nature as a guide to human action can also be problematic for other reasons. Naturalism can involve individuals projecting their understanding of human society on to nature, perhaps unconsciously, and then using nature to justify their social assumptions. Bookchin himself has argued – paradoxically, in view of his criticism of the deep ecologists – that human society should learn from nature, which, he says, is co-operative and largely rejects hierarchy.

The German author Reiner Grundman noted: 'We find it in conservative authors like [Herbert] Gruhl; in Stalinist-Communist countries; and in ecosocialist writers like [Brice] Lalonde. All claim the authority of nature and her laws to be the foundation stone of a new society that will solve ecological problems. Gruhl and [Wolfgang] Harich are alike in that they stress the iron necessity with which nature operates; from this they derive tough political measures. Bookchin argues that spontaneity in life converges with spontaneity in nature, and Lalonde stresses the fact that nature is, and society should be, self-organizing... each version of nature... [is] a construction of its author.'[7]

While it is relatively easy to sketch out some underlying principles that most greens share, such as respect for nature, holism and limits, there are tensions and differences. Greens – like conservatives, socialist, anarchists, feminists or any other political category – disagree with each other when it comes to a number of key ideas. Green politics can be divided between ecoanarchists, ecosocialists, ecofeminists and other groups. In turn, the different variants of green politics are internally divided and sometimes overlap – left biocentrics, for example, seek to label themselves as both socialists and deep ecologists.

Some have argued that these labels are largely irrelevant and see green politics as an ideology that rejects previous political assumptions in favor of a set of new and distinct ideas. Such 'green-greens' also argue that 'green politics is neither left nor right but ahead'. Virtually all greens would argue that the left-right division cannot usefully be applied to green politics. If left-right divisions are based on attitudes towards redistribution of wealth and income, this does not on its own say anything about the all-important distinction between ecocentric and more human-centered approaches. It also ignores the distinction between centralist and decentralist approaches to power – many on the left have believed in redistribution of income and wealth but at the same supported the centralization of power in a stronger state. People on the Left or the Right may have little to say about the issues of limits and holism or animal rights.

Nonetheless, to say that greens are 'neither left nor right' is a little simplistic as well. Clearly, greens are almost always on the political left in that they proclaim the need for social justice and, as we shall see in later chapters, generally advocate anti-corporate, anti-capitalist and left-wing policies. While the left-right division is insufficient to define green politics fully, it is also too important to ignore, given that distribution of wealth and the workings of capitalism have huge implications for the environment, let alone the other pillars of green politics. Intriguingly, the slogan 'neither left nor right' was coined by Herbert Gruhl, a former German Christian Democrat, who joined the Greens, only to leave and found his own conservative Ecology Party, the Ecological Democrats (ODP).

Ecoanarchism
Various forms of ecoanarchism have been important to green politics. The most prominent green anarchist was Murray Bookchin. Bookchin, originally a Marxist from New York, became an anarchist in the 1940s and, using the pseudonym Lewis Herber, wrote about the environmental crisis in the 1950s and 1960s. As we have already noted, he challenged deep ecology and advocated a politics of social ecology. He was instrumental in forming the Left Green

Network in the US. He believed that hierarchical societies dominated by élites were the main cause of environmental destruction. He challenged capitalism and advocated 'libertarian municipalism' – this was the idea that direct democracy via town hall meetings could be used to create a decentralized green society. He tended to engage in polemical arguments with other radical greens, attacking deep ecologists, ecosocialists and other anarchists with intellectual vigor. However, despite his prickly personality that tended to alienate even his allies, he was certainly one of the most important green political thinkers of the 20th century.

Other ecoanarchists have adopted many of Bookchin's ideas but have taken a more flexible approach. Green anarchism, via the decentralist strain, has to some extent influenced nearly all green political thought. Anarchists such as Peter Kropotkin can be seen as early green thinkers. Kropotkin, a 19th-century Russian geographer, took a keen interest in nature. His book *Mutual Aid*, which influenced Bookchin's work, set out to challenge the Social Darwinist view that nature was based on fierce competition, leading to the survival of the fittest. Kropotkin showed

---

The principles of social ecology

Social ecology rests on several related premises:

• Humans are part of nature, but have a unique social awareness.
• The environmental crisis is a result of the hierarchical power structures at the heart of our society.
• These power structures damage humans at least as much as they do the environment.
• By basing society on ecological principles our relationship with nature will be transformed.
• These ecological principles are egalitarian and based on mutual aid, caring and communitarian values.
• This transformation is to be achieved through radical collective action and co-operative social movements.

Source: www.thegreenfuse.org/se-crit.htm

---

that different species often interacted co-operatively. Another of his works, which was important from the point of view of green politics, was *Fields, Factories and Workshops*, which developed practical ideas for localized, communal economies that produced with respect for the natural environment. Kropotkin was one of the sources of inspiration for the Early Green Politics of the late 19th and early 20th centuries.

Ecoanarchists are often strongly anti-capitalist, a position shared in particular with ecosocialists. The important ecosocialist thinker Joel Kovel, for example, who co-authored the Ecosocialist manifesto, worked with Bookchin, learned from him and, like so many others, fell out with him! Not all anarchism is green – some anarchist thinkers were productivists who stressed growth and the expansion of industry with little thought for nature. Anarchism, like any other ideology, is also internally differentiated – there are, for example, both anarcho-communists and anarcho-capitalists. Primitivist and lifestyle anarchists have green sympathies but have been criticized by other green anarchists. Green anarchism is a rich and important field, which could merit a book in its own right.

Ecosocialism

The term 'ecosocialism' also embraces a very important and diverse set of ideas, which along with ecofeminism, requires more detailed discussion than can be fully provided here. In essence, ecosocialists argue that green politics makes most sense when it is on the left. They believe that capitalism, which thrives on increasing production and consumption for profit, is the key driver of ecological destruction.

John Bellamy Foster, in his book *Marx's Ecology*, argues that Marx and his co-writer Friedrich Engels were concerned with environmental issues, including soil erosion, air pollution, food additives and deforestation. There are clearly shared philosophical themes. Marx's ideas stress a holistic network approach, which is highly ecological. Critics of ecosocialism argue, in contrast, that Marx's emphasis on industrial development is highly unecological and point to the poor environmental record of the Soviet Union and other states claiming to follow his ideas. Ecosocialists point to other examples of environmentally conscious socialists such as William Morris and, more recently, Fidel Castro.

An Ecosocialist International Network is active in many parts of the world but most especially Latin America. There are also ecosocialist networks in some Green parties, for example, Green Left in the UK.

Some ecosocialists are less concerned with discussing the green credentials of previous socialist thinkers than with stressing the destructive effects of capitalism on the global environment.

Ecofeminism

Many greens have argued that green politics is intrinsically feminist, and certainly there is considerable overlap between ecofeminism, ecoanarchism and ecosocialism. Important ecofeminists have included the late German Green leader Petra Kelly and the Indian scientist and global justice campaigner Vandana Shiva. Ecofeminists argue that the worst male traits of aggression and fierce competition are behind the excesses of capitalism and drive war. The anti-nuclear power campaigns of the 1970s and the peace movement of the 1980s both drew heavily on feminist thought. The women-only peace camp at Greenham Common in Berkshire in the UK during the 1980s was set up to oppose cruise missile deployment and became a talisman for peace movements worldwide.

Ecofeminists argue that domestic work, generally undertaken by women – including the essential tasks of caring for the old, the sick and children – is undervalued. Green parties have strongly supported feminist policies challenging gender inequality and aiming to improve the status of women. Ecofeminists are passionate critics of a male-dominated society, which they believe is destroying nature:

'We as a species are in an arrested state of adolescence as insecure egos (mostly male) compete for unrestrained power and attention. Playing god, they manipulate life by splicing genes in a frenzy of womb envy. As profit-driven warmongers, they traffic in death.'[8]

Some feminists argue that to suggest that nature is female, and that women are intrinsically more caring and nurturing than men, risks being sexist. This courts the danger that biology is seen as destiny, with women consigned to caring roles. There are a number of complex and important feminist debates in this area, but all feminists argue that a patriarchal society is destructive of nature.

Ecofascism

As well as ecosocialism, ecofeminism and ecoanarchism, none of which are very far from core green political beliefs, there is also ecofascism, which is, to say the least, more difficult to see as part of green politics. The very notion of ecofascism can be challenged as an obvious oxymoron, perhaps as valid as vodka-based teetotalism or hot ice. Ecofascism is often used as an abusive term, particularly by those who themselves are on the right of the political spectrum. Environmental concern is attacked as an authoritarian assault on the right to hunt animals or use a gasoline-guzzling SUV. Given that the second pillar of green politics is social justice and few, if any, greens advocate social injustice, it is difficult to conceive of any fascism, which is based on inequality and conflict, as green. Greens also, to a greater or lesser extent, advocate grassroots democracy rather than the central dictatorial authority beloved of Hitler, Mussolini and their 21st-century followers.

Nonetheless, ecofascism, even if it is rejected as part

of the green political spectrum, exists and advocates a distinct philosophical approach. Ecofascism is not a major phenomenon but thinkers, past and present, such as Jorian Jenks, Knut Hamsun and Pentti Linkola can be described as ecofascists with little dispute.

Jenks, a prominent supporter of organic agriculture, was a well-known member of the British Union of Fascists. He was so central to the organization that its leader Oswald Mosley at one time named him as his replacement in the event that he should die or be imprisoned. Other British ecofascists, like Rolf Gardiner, who established the Springhead Trust in Dorset in the 1930s, were encouraged by the support for organic agriculture provided by Walther Dare, Hitler's farming minister. Hamsun, a Norwegian who won the Nobel Prize for Literature in 1920, wrote lyrical accounts of nature such as *The Growth of the Soil*, was a keen supporter of National Socialism and enjoyed meeting Hitler. The Finnish poet Pentti Linkola combines a reverence for nature with some highly authoritarian views. Linkola sees overpopulation as the key source of environmental damage and has made some extreme statements praising, for example, the virtues of the Holocaust.[9]

It is somewhat difficult to know whether Linkola is serious or merely being provocative when he makes antisemitic, pro-Hitler and other racist statements. However, while there are clearly ecofascist individuals, there is little evidence of organized ecofascist political parties or networks.

The Earth and the spirit

Another area of controversy is the link between green politics and spirituality. For many greens, their outlook has a spiritual dimension. Greens reject mindless materialism and believe that human needs are diverse. Abraham Maslow's hierarchy of needs and post-materialist ideas can be linked to green politics;

he argued that human needs include emotional and spiritual elements as well as the material need for goods.

Many greens believe that humanity once valued the natural world as sacred. Yet the world has lost its enchantment for most of us and we abuse it. Fritjof Capra and Charlene Spretnak have argued that a more spiritual outlook, which saw nature as embodying the sacred, was overtaken by mechanistic ideas that portrayed the universe and life as a set of systems of clockwork, which can be dissected and investigated, during the 16th and 17th centuries. They argue that Francis Bacon, René Descartes and Isaac Newton introduced a reductionist view of nature based on domination and control. This change in philosophy paved the way for an accelerating assault on nature by a humanity armed with powerful technologies.

Other greens argue that Christianity, Islam and Judaism are at the root of our onslaught upon the Earth. All three religions share the Old Testament as a central text, including the proclamation in Genesis that humanity should have dominion over the rest of nature. The ecological ill-effects of the Christian religion were the subject of particular study by the American thinker Lynn White Jr.

In contrast, many Christians, Jews and Muslims have argued that their religious teachings advocate ecological stewardship. In Judaism there are notions of land stewardship. Christianity preaches compassion, nonviolence and justice, and offers the example of St Francis of Assisi, who cared both for the poor and for nature. The Qur'an contains powerful statements that call for humanity to care for the Earth and to reject wasteful overconsumption. The idea of natural balance and harmony is fundamental to Eastern religions such as Buddhism and Taoism. Pagan and indigenous traditions tend to be based on the idea that nature is sacred.

Green philosophy

Ecosocialists have been criticized for failing to recognize this spiritual dimension in their insistence that material forces of social class and economic structure shape our profound beliefs and condition how we treat the natural environment. However, perhaps even ecosocialists have a place for spirituality. Marx dealt with the issue of alienation and the negative effects of our separation from the rest of nature. In Latin America, indigenous politicians such as the Bolivian President Evo Morales see no contradiction between advocating ecosocialism and praising 'Pachamama', the Mother Earth.

Clearly to a greater or lesser extent green politics is about seeing intrinsic value in nature, and another

Ten commandments to save the planet

First, if we want to save the planet earth to save life and humanity, we are obliged to end the capitalist system. The grave effects of climate change, of the energy, food and financial crises, are not a product of human beings in general, but rather of the capitalist system as it is, inhuman, with its idea of unlimited industrial development.

Second, to renounce war, because the people do not win in war, but only the imperial powers; the nations do not win, but rather the transnational corporations. Wars benefit a small group of families and not the people. The trillions of dollars used for war should be directed to repair and cure Mother Earth wounded by climate change.

Third proposal for debate: a world without imperialism or colonialism. Our relationships should be oriented to the principle of complementarity, and to take into account the profound asymmetries that exist family to family, country to country, and continent to continent.

And the fourth point is oriented to the issue of water, which ought to be guaranteed as a human right to avoid its privatization into few hands, given that water is life.

As the fifth point, I would like to say that we need to end the energy debacle. In 100 years we are using up fossil energies created during millions of years. As some presidents are setting aside lands for luxury automobiles and not for human beings, we need to implement policies to impede the use of agro-fuels and in this way to avoid hunger and misery for our peoples.

As a sixth point: the capitalist system treats Mother Earth as a raw material, but the Earth cannot be understood as a commodity;

strain of green thought posits the notion of 'Gaia'. The scientist James Lovelock, in his 1979 book *Gaia: A New Look at Life on Earth*, argued that the Earth is a distinct entity, which uses feedback mechanisms to maintain life. However, the notion that the planet is a living organism – a goddess, perhaps – is somewhat of a minority view in the green movement. Gaia does not tend to be a feature of Green party manifestos, leaflets from green direct action groups such as the Climate Camp or reports from environmental pressure groups such as Friends of the Earth.

Indeed, despite the issues raised in this chapter, Green parties and environmental pressure groups are not generally marked by their deep discussions of green

---

who could privatize, rent or lease their own mother? I propose that we organize an international movement in defense of Mother Nature, in order to recover the health of Mother Earth and re-establish a harmonious and responsible life with her.

A central theme as the seventh point for debate is that basic services, whether they be water, electricity, education or health, need to be taken into account as human rights.

As the eighth point, to consume what is needed, prioritize what we produce and consume locally, end consumerism, decadence and luxury. We need to prioritize local production for local consumption, stimulating self-reliance and the sovereignty of the communities within the limits that the health and remaining resources of the planet permit.

As the next to last point, to promote the diversity of cultures and economies. To live in unity respecting our differences, not only physical, but also economic, through economies managed by the communities and their associations.

Sisters and brothers, as the tenth point, we propose to Live Well – not live better at the expense of another, but Live Well based on the lifestyle of our peoples, the riches of our communities, fertile lands, water and clean air. Socialism is talked about a lot, but we need to improve this socialism, improve the proposals for socialism in the 21st century, building a communitarian socialism, or simply Live Well, in harmony with Mother Earth, respecting the shared life ways of the community. ■

Bolivian President Evo Morales, 9 October 2008
http://climateandcapitalism.com/?p=566

philosophy. The threat of climate change has prompted a demand for urgent solutions. In some parts of the world, the greens have gone from being a marginal force to acting as major political players. Such changes have led to less emphasis on philosophical debate and more concern with practical politics.

While green philosophy has been 'ecocentric' rather 'anthropocentric', Green parties, particularly in government, have tended to emphasize the benefits of their policies for human beings, as voles and other species don't have votes.

Green politics isn't just about the use of elections or nonviolent direct action to achieve immediate ends, it is also about deep-seated cultural change. Green politics involves us all reconsidering the relationship of our species to the rest of nature. Philosophical debates do have a role, and political strategy depends on the extent to which cultural change occurs in society. However, in a world of new media it is also difficult to advance the more sophisticated ideas that cannot be compressed into an easy soundbite or a tweet. At its best, green politics encourages us to ask some very big questions that are largely ignored by other political ideologies. The answers to those questions are not always simple.

1 Arne Naess, *Ecology, Community and Lifestyle*, Cambridge University Press, 1989. 2 Cited in Joel Kovel, *The Enemy of Nature*, Zed 2002. 3 Elinor Ostrom, speech on accepting induction to the American Academy of Political and Social Science, http://blog.aapss.org/index.cfm?commentID=58 4 www.uwmc.uwc. edu/geography/malthus/sen_NYR.htm 5 Fritjof Capra and Charlene Spretnak, *Green Politics*, Paladin, 1985. 6 Arne Naess, op cit. 7 Reiner Grundman, *Marxism and Ecology*, Clarendon Press, 1991. 8 http://tinyurl.com/yglmyhf 9 See, for example, www.corrupt.org/data/files/pentti_linkola/

4 Need not greed

In a world where conventional economic thinking – based on free-market mechanisms and consumer-led growth – has led us on to the rocks, the interest in green economic alternatives has become more serious and more urgent. From environmental taxes that cost in the damage to the Earth to a basic income that could be provided to all, greens have advanced a range of creative proposals that could lead to a more sustainable future.

GANDHI FAMOUSLY ARGUED that Earth provides enough to satisfy 'everyone's need, but not everyone's greed'. This is a good summary of the green attitude to economics. Greens believe that ever-increasing consumption is neither possible nor desirable. Along with their rejection of economic growth, greens are skeptical of unlimited international trade, globalization and other aspects of conventional economics which are seen as common sense by just about everyone else. The green critique is at its most radical when it comes to economics.

Green economics can even be seen as a heresy. Theodore Roszak, in the concluding chapter of his book *Where the Wasteland Ends*, noted: 'Economy of means and simplicity of life – voluntarily chosen – have always been the secret to fulfillment; while acquisitiveness and extravagance are a despairing waste of life. That ought to be a platitude. In our situation, it is heresy.'[1]

It is difficult to see how ecological systems can be maintained with ever-increasing economic growth. More and more production, consumption and waste tend to lead to increases in greenhouse gases and habitat destruction.

Greens also believe that diminishing resources, particularly peak oil, make economic growth unsustainable. The biologist EO Wilson has argued that if everyone on the planet consumed as much as the average US citizen, we would need five planet Earths. At the moment we consume approximately 80 million barrels of oil a day, and it is difficult to see how supplies of oil can be sustained if the economy keeps expanding. Of course it is possible to run cars on electricity from renewable sources and there are potentially abundant supplies of renewable energy, but it seems unlikely on a planet with finite resources that the economy could grow and grow, upwards and forever.

Advocates of unlimited capitalism argue that supply and demand will make markets work to conserve resources and that technological advances will solve our problems. But markets can have perverse and unintended consequences. As a resource becomes scarcer in the market, it tends to become more expensive. This should encourage people to buy less expensive substitutes. However, it also encourages the over-exploitation of resources. As oil becomes more expensive, there is more incentive for oil exploration and for accelerating its production, which not only reduces the quantity available but also has noxious ecological consequences. With recent rising prices, the exploitation of the tar sands in Canada has become attractive. Extracting oil from these tar sands is hugely wasteful of energy and highly polluting but profit from high prices is seen as more powerful than the motive of conservation.

Even if the economy could continue to grow without ecological damage or exhaustion of resources, greens do not believe that such growth is necessarily desirable. Many studies have suggested that, once certain levels of prosperity have been reached, increasing economic growth does not actually increase human happiness. The focus on economic expansion also leads to society becoming more greedy and competitive. The British academic Richard Layard has argued that, because growth does not lead to increased levels of human satisfaction, we should move to an economy based on the desire to increase human happiness rather than economic growth.[2]

Economic growth is also often linked to increasing inequality. For the economy to grow, new areas of life have to be exploited by the market. Varied human needs are commercialized and used to sell goods – increasingly, everything is up for sale. Economic growth is also fueled by a huge spend on advertising. Advertising is wasteful in itself and can be seen as a way of manufacturing dissatisfaction. More and more needs in a capitalist society are transformed into the need for consumable commodities. To be a good parent, one should work long hours to afford more things for the babies. To be fulfilled sexually requires a huge and diverse industry. The body, created by a lifestyle based on unhealthy food and a sedentary car-based lifestyle, has become a new focus of capitalist growth, with billions spent on diets.[3] Ted Trainer, in his book *Abandon Affluence!* notes: 'Acquiring things is important to many of us today because there is not much else that yields interest and a sense of progress and satisfaction in life.'[4]

Growth does not reduce poverty

It is not even a matter of saying that conventional growth reduces poverty in economically poorer parts of the globe. In 'developing' countries, higher growth levels may paradoxically lead to more poverty through processes that enclose forests and other communal resources. Many communities gather wood to use as fuel or graze their animals on common land; such activity sustains local economies but will not be recorded by GNP or other measures of economic growth. Governments keen to increase growth – and often with shady connections to corporations – may see such local economic activity as backward; often it is invisible to them. Creating economic growth can be a violent process, whereby land is seized, human rights abused and small communities oppressed to create 'development'.

China and India are presently enjoying high economic growth, despite the recent recession. Living standards are growing but the cost of this kind of

---

What is the commons?

For many people in the West, the word 'commons' carries an archaic flavor: that of the medieval village pasture which villagers did not own but where they had rights to graze their livestock. Yet, for the vast majority of humanity, the commons is an everyday reality. Ninety per cent of the world's fishers rely on small inshore marine commons, catching over half the fish eaten in the world today. In the Philippines, Java and Laos, irrigation systems are devised and run by villagers themselves, the water rights being distributed through rules laid down by the community. Even in the North, there are communities which still manage their forests, pastures, fisheries and water supplies jointly.

Moreover, new commons are constantly being born, even among what might seem the most fragmented communities. In the inner cities of the US, the dialects of black communities express concepts that the language taught in state schools cannot touch. In southern California, water users have crafted self-governing institutional structures, basin by basin, and watershed by watershed, to control water abstraction from local aquifers. At toxic dump sites and around proposed nuclear plants in France, Switzerland and elsewhere, people have insisted on their 'rights' to keep the earth and air around their communities free from the threat of poisonous and radioactive substances, damning the economic and 'public' rationality which dictates that their homes are 'objectively' the best locations for waste sinks. For them, the sentiments expressed by an elder of a Brazilian tribe, despite the religious language in which they are couched, cannot be completely unrecognizable:

'The only possible place for the Krenak people to live and to re-establish our existence, to speak to our gods, to speak to our nature, to weave our lives, is where God created us. We can no longer see the planet that we live upon as if it were a chessboard where people just move things around.' ∎

Source: Nicholas Hildyard, Larry Lohmann, Sarah Sexton and Simon Fairlie, 'Reclaiming the Commons', http://tinyurl.com/yjescuj

'progress' is that it actually brings poverty to many people. A good example of this process has occurred at Nandigram in the Indian state of West Bengal, where a Communist Party state government that over many decades has done much for the poor embarked on a Chinese-style strategy of fast industrial development. Land was taken from local peasants for a number of industrial projects, including the construction of a Tata Nana car factory. Peasants claimed that they had been forced to give up their farmland without proper compensation. Claims of repression and human rights abuse followed.

Across the world there are, meanwhile, almost daily accounts of indigenous people being removed to make way for mines and oil exploration. Their stories rarely find their way into the media but show a side to economic growth which is, in a sense, uneconomic, depressing living standards by destroying sustainable local economies that are often based on ecological principles and that maintain sensitive environments.

For all the reasons outlined, greens have argued that measures of economic growth such Gross Domestic Product (GDP) should be replaced with alternative indicators that more accurately measure improvements in human welfare. The Human Development Index, a basket of economic indicators that includes GDP but also life expectancy and literacy rates, is also used to measure standards of living. Invented by the Pakistani economist Mahbub ul Haq, but inspired by the thinking of the Indian economist Amartya Sen, it is more sensitive than GDP and it takes into account many of the criticisms of conventional economics outlined above. Sen, a Nobel Prize winner, argues that development is only possible if human beings can flourish under conditions of real democratic participation, decentralization of power and freedom, including for women.

Taking the critique of conventional notions of

economic growth still further, Bhutan has introduced the notion of 'gross national happiness' as an alternative measure to GDP.

The Bhutan measure may appear naïve and we might ask how you can measure happiness. Yet it is based on some careful research and uses nine sets of categories to measure welfare carefully (see box).

Measuring development using different indicators is a positive initiative, but it does not answer the rather more fundamental question of how to create a truly sustainable economy. Indeed, while the term 'sustainable development' has come into common use, it is often employed to describe attempts to sustain greater economic growth rather than as a token of environmental concern. Sustainable development is, in theory, development that 'meets the needs of the present without compromising the ability of future generations to meet their own needs'. If economic growth is incompatible with meeting the needs of future generations, how can we meet present needs without such growth? This is a very difficult and

---

Gross National Happiness

'A measure of Gross National Happiness might be presumed to comprise a single psychological question on happiness such as "Taking all things together, would you say you are: Very happy, Rather happy, Not very happy, or Not at all happy." Another measure is the subjective well-being measure generated from a question such as "On the scale of one to ten, how would you rate yourself?" One is not a happy person and 10 is a very happy person.

'However, neither of these indicators are good multi-dimensional measures of happiness. The objectives of the kingdom of Bhutan, and the Bhutanese understandings of happiness, are much broader than those that are referred to as "happiness" in the Western literature. Under the title of happiness, we include a range of dimensions of human well-being. Some of these are quite traditional areas of social concern such as living standards, health and education. Some are less traditional, such as time-use, emotional well-being, culture, community vitality, or environmental diversity.' ■

Source: Government of Bhutan, http://tinyurl.com/ycff2pl

---

important question, which most governments are happy to forget about as they pander to the greed of existing populations to fuel more economic growth.

One approach is to decouple prosperity from growth, finding ways of improving the quality of human life without producing ever-increasing quantities of goods and services. This was broadly the approach taken by a ground-breaking report from the Sustainable Development Commission (SDC). The Sustainable Development Commission, which is funded by the UK Government, gathered evidence suggesting, for all the reasons outlined here, that sustainable development was incompatible with continued economic growth. The Commission has suggested a variety of ways to make people better off without growth.

The idea of creating prosperity without growth is easier than it might at first appear. The SDC is keen to emphasize the importance of social goods and services shared by citizens, such as public parks and other community resources. Economic growth does not measure our access to the goods we need but rather how fast we throw things away and buy new ones. If goods can be made to last longer or made easier to repair, this reduces economic growth but it also lessens ecological impact and with it the use of finite resources. If goods last longer, because we don't need to replace them as often, it certainly reduces economic growth but it does not affect our prosperity.

Social sharing

The concept of social sharing, developed by the US legal theorist Yochai Benkler, is a powerful tool for reconciling human development with ecological and resource limits and looks likely to revolutionize our understanding of economics over the next few decades.[5] Normally, we are aware of two kinds of property: private property, where individuals own resources and goods; and state property, as with

Need not greed

National Health Service hospitals in Britain that are owned by the government. Benkler argues that there is another category of resources that can be owned collectively. Such collective ownership can give more people greater access to the things they need without the duplication of private ownership. Libraries, although they are usually provided by the state, are perhaps the best illustration of this. If there are libraries full of books that individuals can borrow, more people can have more access to the books they want. Without libraries, if we had to buy and privately own every book we wanted, there would be more books in print but much less access.

Benkler believes that, for many items, spare capacity exists. We may want personally to own a particular book and consult it every day. However, it seems pointless to own a book we might only want to read once – so why not borrow it instead? Spare capacity exists, so even with fewer books printed, we can use them as much as we want. Car clubs are another example of social sharing. These might be run by the private sector for profit, but they allow us access to a variety of vehicles, so that some of us who might only use a car on occasion can avail ourselves of the facility without having to buy our own vehicle. Social sharing does not abolish private property but it does mean that we can consume fewer things, because, for many goods and services, one person's use of an object or service does not preclude its use later by others. Social sharing could be extended to all sorts of goods and services. It would certainly reduce the use of scarce resources and cut our ecological impact – yet by improving access it would also boost what we might call 'sustainable prosperity'.

Social sharing already exists but is often forgotten. Most indigenous land is communal – access to it is social as long as ecological limits are respected. It is vital to maintain such communal forms of ecological land ownership from assaults by oil companies, mining corporations, loggers and agribusiness. Social sharing also dominates the knowledge economy, with the internet allowing for the creation of free and open-source software. When you download Firefox as a web browser rather than Microsoft's equivalent, you are freely accessing software that has been developed by a global online community of volunteers who have given their own time and ingenuity. When you look something up on Wikipedia you are again benefiting from the idealistic commitment and freely given time of volunteers worldwide who see this knowledge as part of a 'global commons' rather than as something that should be bought and sold.

Green economics, by challenging growth, tends to subvert capitalism. If we produce and consume less, profits fall for corporations, large companies move into recession and economic activity becomes increasingly free and democratic. While this might seem like a wild statement to make, the decline of corporate media and the rise of free software and downloading is a good illustration of how the formal capitalist economy is being transformed by systems of social sharing.

The success of Elinor Ostrom, who has spent decades researching the commons as a way of conserving the environment, illustrates the growing importance of the economics of sharing. In 2009 Ostrom became the first woman to win the Nobel Prize for Economics – though, in view of her field of study, it was perhaps appropriate that she shared the prize with another economist.

Some argue that social sharing is compatible with capitalist markets. Capitalists can continue to do business despite reduced economic activity and changes in ownership patterns. While not necessarily an example of green economies, the very fact that many of us rent mobile phones rather than buying them outright

Need not greed

is a good illustration of the revolution in attitudes to property and ownership that is sweeping the economy. I am skeptical personally that a green capitalism, which substitutes one-off ownership for forms of rent, is possible. Can capitalism survive while we consume less? This seems impossible given capitalism's traditional reliance on rising consumption.

Localism

Ecosocialists are critical of markets in general, feeling that they are based on exclusion and inefficiency, and that they generate unnecessary waste. However, this is too radical for many others in the green movement. An alternative perspective comes from the US writer David Korten, who argues that, while greens must be anti-capitalist, they should also embrace markets. He believes that if markets are localized they work to promote ecological values, social justice and democracy. Korten believes – like Adam Smith, supposedly the father of free-market economics – that the growth of monopolistic corporations is the source of the negative features of capitalism. If markets are genuinely based on competition and consumers can choose between different firms, business will have to act to serve consumers. However, in markets where just one or a small number of firms dominate, consumers will

---

Seven generations

'I am deeply indebted to the indigenous peoples in the US, who had an image of seven generations being the appropriate time to think about the future. I think we should all reinstate in our mind the seven-generation rule. When we make really major decisions, we should ask not only what will it do for me today, but what will it do for my children, my children's children, and their children's children into the future.' ■

Elinor Ostrom, winner of the 2009 Nobel Prize for Economics for her work on 'the commons'.

Source: http://blog.aapss.org/index.cfm?commentID=58

---

be exploited. A monopoly is bad for both workers and the environment. Korten points to the growth of monopolistic markets in virtually all important areas of the economy.[6]

Corporations are increasingly transnational. This means they gain even more power and can disregard environmental regulations by moving to countries where standards are lax. By relocating to countries where labor costs are low, they can push down wages globally; they also tend to have the effect of moving the tax burden on to consumers while lowering government spending on services such as healthcare. To Korten and most other greens, transnationals are a menace. By operating globally and increasingly shifting goods from one side of the globe to the other, they also accelerate climate change by creating ever more unnecessary emissions.

Korten believes that transnationals have an increasingly powerful political role, along with other instruments of neoliberal globalization such as the International Monetary Fund and the World Trade Organization, and the increasingly free movement of currency. Corporate-friendly globalization pushes countries into adopting policies which hurt the poor and wreck the environment. For example, if a nation-state protects workers with strong union rights or increases corporation tax, transnationals will move somewhere else. Transnational corporations have a great deal of power over governments, which they exercise by threatening to remove their investment.

Korten and other green localists believe that markets can be made to work if the corporations are broken up and more economic activity occurs locally. Korten's ideas are close to those of the Hungarian writer and thinker Karl Polanyi, who argued in his 1944 book *The Great Transformation*, that markets, if their ill-effects are to be minimized, need to be embedded in strong local communities.[7] If we can see how the goods we consume are produced, abuse of the environment and workers is far less likely. Such localization also links to the green rejection of economic globalization. Greens believe that globalization leads to increased poverty for many and increases massively the power and wealth of those who already dominate society.

Greens are also critical of unlimited international trade. While greens certainly don't want to ban international trade, they do see some very major ill-effects that flow from the prevailing emphasis on international exchange. Like the green critique of growth, this seems at first both radical and even a little bizarre. Surely trade between different nations has to be beneficial…?

Greens believe that increasing international trade

The Green New Deal

Britain's Green New Deal Group drew inspiration from the tone of President Roosevelt's comprehensive response to the Great Depression to propose a modernized economy designed to power a renewables revolution, create thousands of green-collar jobs and rein in the distorting power of the finance sector while making more low-cost capital available for pressing priorities.

1 **A massive environmental transformation of the economy to tackle the triple crunch of the financial crisis, climate change and insecure energy supplies.**

2 **Jobs, more jobs and secure jobs.** And it's about the skills and training to create and sustain them: in a time of recession, with unemployment already rocketing in the US, and growing here, shifting to green energy will produce countless new jobs, and create many more pound-for-pound of investment, than propping up the current system.

3 **Investment now to tackle the current recession, and an investment for the future.** There are lots of ways we can invest in the future… public spending on a green new deal will reap economic, environmental and social benefits. We can spend 'better' by reforming taxes, so that we tax more what we want less of (like pollution and reckless speculation) and less what we want more of (like green goods and services). Investment can come from public and private sources, as well as our savings. Shutting tax havens and ensuring that corporate tax reporting accurately reflects profits made in a country, would raise billions more

is not simply an 'apple pie benefit' that is always for the good. Caroline Lucas, presently the leader of the Green Party of England and Wales, and the late Mike Woodin, a former Green Party Principal Speaker, put forward the case against unlimited international trade in their book *Green Alternatives to Globalization*.[8] They note that international trade may lead to the exploitation of producers with less market power. Globalization may lead to a race to the bottom, with companies forced to cut wages, working conditions and environmental protection to minimize costs. Extreme competitive pressure makes sense within the framework of traditional economics but is damaging in social and environmental terms.

Where trade accelerates economic activity, it often

---

for public investment in both rich and poor countries.

4 New checks, balances and directions for a banking system that has become unfit for purpose. Everyone agrees that new rules are needed to prevent a repeat of the banks' catastrophic errors, but there's also a new opportunity for change. With the taxpayer now owning several banks, we can make sure that they invest and lend at low, affordable interest rates to support the economy's environmental transformation.

5 Greater security for our pensions and savings. Many people's pensions have taken a battering, but now there's a chance to create new, low-risk steady-return vehicles for saving. New bonds and pensions targeted at the green renewal of the nation's infrastructure could help bring mutual long-term benefits to both savers and the nation as a whole.

6 Warm homes in winter, protecting us from high and volatile energy prices and ending fuel poverty. Too many people can't afford to keep warm in winter. Whatever the international price of fuel, homeowners seem to have to pay ever higher prices. A Green New Deal will begin by improving insulation and energy efficiency in UK households and start to break our dependence on volatile, expensive and ultimately declining fossil fuels.

7 The Green New Deal is about setting the economy, nationally and globally, on a path to live within its environmental means. It is also about fair play in a warming world and calls for the new financial mechanisms to help the Majority World adapt to climate change as well as breaking the carbon chains of fossil-fuel dependence. ∎

damages the environment, Edward Goldsmith and Jerry Mander noted with some bitterness:

> 'By now, it should be clear that our environment is becoming ever less capable of sustaining the growing impact of our economic activities. Everywhere our forests are overlogged, our agricultural lands overcropped, our grasslands overgrazed, our wetlands overdrained, our groundwaters overtapped, our seas overfished, and nearly all our terrestrial and marine environment is overpolluted with chemical and radioactive poisons [...] In such conditions, there can only be one way of maintaining the habitability of our planet, and that is to set out to reduce the impact. Unfortunately, the overriding goal of just about every government in the world is to maximise this impact through economic globalization.'[9]

As has already been observed, green economics has a strong social element, recognizing that capitalism creates inequality and injustice. Greens, like socialists, are strongly committed to creating a more equal world. Greens reject solutions to environmental problems that increase inequality. For example, many greens believe in a carbon tax or other charges that turn environmental costs into taxes so as to discourage pollution. However, such taxes take a greater proportion of the incomes of those who are on low incomes and have often been supported by right-wing politicians as a way of shifting the tax burden from the well off and corporations on to the backs of poorer citizens. To avoid such consequences, greens believe that other indirect taxes – especially purchase or sales taxes – should be reduced. The climate scientist James Hansen believes that a carbon tax would be more effective than the dubious use of carbon trading in reducing emissions but it might be combined with dividend payments to prevent it hitting poorer citizens. Equally, without investment in insulation and better public transport, environmental taxation will be unjust. Policies that protect the environment but harm those who are less well off cannot really be considered 'green'.

Green economics is also feminist. Domestic labor is still usually undertaken by women and is normally unpaid. Women suffer from lower incomes and less wealth than men. Maria Mies, the green feminist economist, has used the concept of a pyramid to suggest that conventional economics fails to take into account the most important economic activity often undertaken by women and wrongly puts formal monetized economics first. The top of Mies's pyramid, which is measured by GNP, includes conventional economic activity; the middle of the pyramid includes food production by peasants – often women – which is not monetized because production and consumption occur at local level without cash trade; while near the

A feeling for the forest

'First, the sensibility I gained from living with the forest, from being born there and taking my sustenance from it until I was 16 years old. Second was my contact with liberation theology, with people like Chico Mendes, a connection that raised social and political consciousness about the actions of the Amazonian rubber-tappers and Indians who were being driven out of their lands because the old rubber estates were being turned into cattle ranches. These encounters made me become engaged with the struggle in defense of the forest. Later, I discovered that this was about "the environment" and the protection of ecosystems. It was an ethical commitment that these natural resources could not be simply destroyed.' ■

Marina Silva, the Brazilian Green Party Presidential candidate discusses how she became environmentally aware.

Source: *Washington Post*, 20 November 2009.

bottom of the pyramid comes domestic labor, usually provided for free by women; and at the very bottom of the pyramid is nature, which provides all we need. Maria Mies talks of subsistence economics. By this she means the economic activity that allows the human race to continue in existence – the work of women and the contribution of nature are vital to this but tend to be ignored.

Mies calls for an ecofeminist revolution to save nature and to raise women to their proper place in society. She uses the term 'subsistence perspective' to describe her ecofeminist economics. The subsistence perspective stresses the goals of life – in contrast to the goal of capitalism, which is to accumulate more profit through growth.

> 'A lot of people ask: what do you mean by subsistence? I usually say: for us, subsistence is the opposite of commodity production. Commodity production is the goal of capitalist production – in other words, a general production of goods, everything that there is, has to be transformed into a commodity. It is possible to observe that today, especially in the course of globalization. Subsistence production has an entirely different goal, namely, the direct satisfaction of human needs. This isn't accomplished through money and the production of goods. For us, quite essential is that it is a direct production and reproduction of life. That's why we talk of "life production" rather than "commodity production".'[10]

Greens variously emphasize the feminist, socialist and localist elements of green economics. Some greens stress the need to turn external costs into internal prices. This approach treats environmental damage as an uncosted element in the market. If costed and included in prices, it is argued that it would lead to a green economy. Those green taxes and charges can be seen as an element of the green economic vision. However, as we have noted, these taxes tend to have a greater impact on poorer people and don't challenge the growth imperative of capitalism. This is why most greens believe in more radical reforms and argue that taxes need to be balanced with redistribution or the promotion of practical alternatives if they are to have a positive effect.

Basic income

In their efforts to redistribute income and to support vital but often non-monetized aspects of the economic system such as caring, many greens back the concept of a basic income scheme. This is the idea, similar to a negative income tax, that all members of society should be paid a regular, perhaps weekly or monthly, sum of money. This would redistribute to the poor and guarantee that everyone in society has access to a basic income so as to provide for essential needs. Those who wished to do less formal work would be supported, so it would subsidize and support carers and others who want to live in ways that are less dependent on the formal growth economy. Greens are keen to advocate redistribution of this kind since, if the economy cannot grow forever, inequality becomes much less desirable.

Green investment in renewable energy and improved public transport infrastructure would create millions of new jobs but in a green economy there would be far less formal work. Greens are also keen to redistribute work via work sharing. The French Green Party, when it participated in a coalition government with the Left, pushed strongly for a reduction in the working week to 35 hours so as to encourage a more equal distribution of work.

Need not greed

A green basic incomes scheme would also encourage 'prosuming'. This word, coined by the French radical Andre Gorz, is a combination of production and consumption activity. By providing workshops, computer facilities and other equipment, the distinction between production and consumption could be blurred, because advances in technology would make it increasingly easy for us to produce many goods in a personalized way. We could make more of the things we need to reflect the features we like.

Small is beautiful

Greens to varying degrees also advocate monetary reform. The creation of credit by private banks allows them to make new money, essentially out of thin air, that they can lend out as debt. This allows banks to expand the supply of money and profit from interest at the same time. While the idea that money is no longer based on assets with intrinsic value, and can just be created out of nothing, seems rather astonishing, it is increasingly acknowledged by conventional economists. In Britain during the recent recession, the Bank of England used the jargonistic term 'quantitative easing' to describe its creation of new money it could inject into the system. Green monetary reformers argue that such a process could be used to fund green projects such as renewable energy. Other greens are more cautious, believing that such credit creation could reduce faith in money and have inflationary consequences. It is a little too easy to think that printing more cash and spending it could solve all of our problems. However, the need for radical reform of banking and finance is supported by all greens. Green economics may generally be perceived as on the left but it rejects the traditional socialist emphasis on central planning that can be bureaucratic and undemocratic. The green opposition to centralized structures was developed strongly by the economist

EF Schumacher in his book *Small is Beautiful: A Study of Economics as if People Mattered.*

> 'I was brought up on the theory of "economies of scale" that with industries and firms, just as with nations, there is an irresistible trend, dictated by modern technology, for units to become ever bigger... Small-scale organization allows for greater flexibility and human communication; in short, decentralized economic activity allows for the convenience, humanity, and manageability of smallness.' Schumacher stresses the need to be able to hold 'seemingly opposite necessities of truth', noting that 'we suffer from an almost universal idolatry of gigantism... For every activity there is a certain appropriate scale.'[11]

Green localists stress that markets can be tamed by local control, while ecosocialists are more skeptical and believe that markets have a built-in tendency to take from the poor and to give to the rich, leading to the growth of monopoly. The idea that green economics should be based on co-operatives and mutuals that are owned and run democratically by workers is something common to different parts of the green movement. The extension of social sharing and the commons is seen as a way of providing prosperity without growth. This is a strong aspect of both ecosocialist and ecofeminist economics. Greens believe in higher income and corporation taxes to redistribute from rich to poor. They also generally advocate effective publicly provided services like the current British National Health Service. For this reason, the US Green Party has strongly supported healthcare reform, believing that the present US system, based on private insurance, inevitably leaves many in society without adequate healthcare. Different strands of green economic thinking generally support the need for some central control and state provision of services such as healthcare, postal services and public transport.

This brief survey shows that greens pretty much turn the logic of conventional economics upside down. Growth, international trade, economies of scale and markets are all treated critically – they do not automatically work to benefit us. The green alternative is dizzyingly different. The bank crisis and subsequent recession has eroded faith in the conventional analysis. There is a heightened awareness that accelerated growth through extending the free market, far from leading to prosperity, has created chaos. The key assumptions of conventional economic analysis – ever-increasing growth, profit and production – seem increasingly difficult to sustain. Green economics looks increasingly likely to shape our future. Indeed, if humanity is to have a future beyond rising inequality and climate chaos, green economics will need to be introduced as a practical set of policies. Neoliberalism has failed – and along with it have perished many of the former certainties of traditional economic analysis.

1 Theodore Roszak, *Where the Wasteland Ends*, Doubleday, New York, 1972. **2** Richard Layard, *Happiness*, Penguin, London, 2006. **3** Erich Fromm, *To Have Or To Be*, Abacus, London, 1979. **4** Ted Trainer, *Abandon Affluence!* cited in Andrew Dobson, *The Green Reader*, Andre Deutsch, London, 1991. **5** Yochai Benkler, *The Wealth of Networks: How Social Production Transforms Markets and Freedom*, Yale University Press, 2006. **6** David Korten, *When corporations rule the world*, Berrett-Koehler, San Francisco, 1995. **7** Karl Polanyi, *The Great Transformation: the political and economic origins of our time*, Beacon Press, Boston, 1944. **8** Michael Woodin and Caroline Lucas, *Green Alternatives to Globalization*, Pluto Press, London, 2004. **9** Edward Goldsmith and Jerry Mander, *The Case Against the Global Economy – and for a turn towards localization*, Earthscan, London, 2001. **10** www.republicart.net/disc/aeas/mies01_en.htm **11** EF Schumacher, *Small is Beautiful: A Study of Economics as if People Mattered*, Blond & Briggs, London, 1973.

5 Politics for life

Green parties are often accused of being focused on a single issue – the environment. Yet their policy platforms cover every aspect of modern life. Here is a brief and inevitably sweeping survey of key ideas advanced by Green parties the world over.

GREEN PARTY POLICIES flow from core green values of ecology, social justice, peace and grassroots democracy. Yet such policies are shaped by political circumstances and vary, at least a little, from one part of the world to another. Green parties have very strong environmental policies, of course, and are particularly keen to create a carbon-free future. As a consequence, they are often accused of being single-issue parties, but actually their policies cover the whole political agenda.

Renewable energy
Energy policy is of particular and urgent importance because of climate change and other forms of damage caused by the burning of fossil fuels. Greens essentially aim for a zero carbon economy, supporting the use of a wide range of renewable energy sources. Wind, wave, tidal, geothermal and solar will all make a vital contribution to a sustainable future but Greens are aware that even renewable energy can have an environmental impact. For example, the Green Party of England and Wales has rejected plans for a tidal barrage across the Severn Estuary because of the effect this would have on local wading bird populations. Greens in New Zealand/Aotearoa, meanwhile, have been involved in opposing large-scale and inappropriate wind farms in particularly sensitive landscapes. Big dam projects in much of the world have led to the displacement of communities whose homes have been flooded, so even hydroelectric power projects are treated with some caution. The first Green

87

political party, in Tasmania, Australia, was formed as a result of a campaign against the Lake Pedder dam's flooding of an area of important tropical forest.

There is a dilemma around the issue of scale. Larger renewable-energy projects are likely to have a more negative environmental impact but at the same time tend to be far more effective at generating energy because of the potential for economies of scale. Despite criticism of wind farms because of their visual quality, most Green parties are keen advocates of wind energy generation. Greens would massively invest in renewable energy and roll out large scale conservation measures such as home insulation to reduce energy demand. Simply using less

Wind power takes off

Global wind power capacity reached 94,100 megawatts by the end of 2007, up 27 per cent on the previous year, and then topped 100,000 megawatts by April 2008. New wind installations were second only to natural gas in the United States as an additional source of power capacity and were the leading source of new capacity in the European Union. ■

Source: Janet L Sawin, 'Wind Power continues rapid rise', Apr 2008, Worldwatch Institute, Vital Signs http://vitalsigns.worldwatch.org/

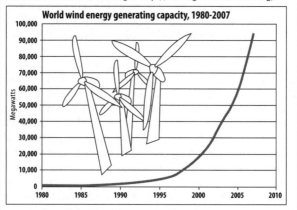

World wind energy generating capacity, 1980-2007

energy by cutting waste is the easiest and cheapest way of reducing CO_2 emissions. European Greens propose a European Union-wide energy grid so that electricity produced from solar, wind, waves and other renewables could be transmitted across the continent to balance demand. This would remove the problem of depending on renewables that are influenced by changes in the weather and could guarantee clean energy supply. When the wind isn't blowing in Yorkshire, energy from another source in another part of Europe could make up the shortfall.

While they believe that some energy can be produced from waste, the policy of growing biofuels is generally rejected by Green parties. The fastest growing source of biofuels is palm oil and demand for biofuels for vehicles in the European Union and North America is accelerating rainforest destruction. The increasing use of biofuels has also led to increased food prices, as land that could have been used for food crops is effectively hijacked to feed cars instead. Biofuels tend to make people hungry as a cost of maintaining car use.

Greens reject nuclear power as inherently dangerous. The Green Party of England and Wales notes that it is 'fundamentally opposed to nuclear energy, which we consider to be expensive and dangerous. The technology is not carbon neutral and, being reliant on uranium, it is not renewable. We consider its use, moreover, to be élitist and undemocratic. There is so far no safe way of disposing of nuclear waste. To a degree unequaled by even the worst of other dangerous industries, the costs and dangers of nuclear energy and its waste will be passed on to future generations long after any benefits have been exhausted.'[1]

Getting around

Transport policy is also vital because it is a key driver of climate change and other environmental ills. Vehicle pollution leads to acid rain from nitrous dioxide and sulphur dioxide. The fine particles from vehicle emissions contribute to lung damage. Even if fueled by clean sources of energy, roads for vehicles destroy habitats and have damaging social effects. The building of roads and freeways is a major threat to the environment, irrespective of the fuel used by the vehicles carried. Cars have negative social effects if they make it impossible for children to play outside; they divide communities and reduce the quality of life. Cars need to be made cleaner but Green parties challenge the assumptions of a transport system that makes the car king and sees other forms of transport as second choices.

Flights are one of the fastest-growing sources of greenhouse gases and planes are particularly damaging contributors to climate change because they emit CO_2 and nitrous oxide directly into the upper atmosphere. The noise pollution from aircraft and the ill-effects of building new runways are also negative environmental features of flying. To cut the need for flying and to reduce car dependency, Greens would massively invest in public transport, expanding buses and trains. More fundamentally, however, Greens believe in localizing economic activity so as to reduce transport demand – the more things we source from close to home (or at least from within our own country rather than from the other side of the world), the more we reduce the overall emissions from freight and transport.

The Green Party of England and Wales argues that 'car driving is not a right but a privilege' and seeks to extend cheap rail travel to all citizens so as to cut unnecessary car use. They also advocate shifting freight from roads on to railways. In the US, where public transport is less developed than in Europe, the Green Party advocates a major expansion of the rail network.

Beyond recycling
Green policies on waste also link to climate change. Methane produced from decaying rubbish is 23 times

more powerful as a greenhouse gas than CO_2, so tackling waste is also an effective way of reducing global warming. Landfill and incineration are both highly polluting ways of dealing with waste and even recycling is not a solution in and of itself. Greens tend to believe that the goal should be to reduce waste and to eliminate it altogether wherever possible.

In any society that promoted prosperity without growth, consumer goods would be built to last longer and be capable of repair – instead of, as at present, companies building in obsolescence so that new versions of their products can be bought and sold only a few years down the line. This would result in far fewer items being thrown away. So too would the reuse of products. Among the positive signs on this front are the increasing number of vehicles running on discarded vegetable oil rather than on hydrocarbons – and the increasing incidence of community 'freecycle' days, where people offer goods they no longer need to other members of their community. Where Greens have achieved positions of power they have been able to make eliminating waste a priority, as in San Francisco in 2007, when Supervisor Ross Mirkarimi outlawed non-biodegradable plastic bags.

Recycling of glass, metals, papers and many plastics is perfectly possible and could be instituted on a much more extensive basis than at present, where much depends on the market value of recyclable materials. Organic waste can be used to generate electricity, thereby providing a double benefit in reducing the methane produced if it is dumped in landfill sites.

Some Green parties believe that manufactured items should be made part of a zero waste cycle, so that every component can be reused or recycled. The Green Party of Aotearoa New Zealand advocates an 'extended producer responsibility'. This would mean that the producer of a good must take responsibility for its disposal. A similar policy already exists in the European Union for a number of products, including cars and electronic items. The EU's Waste Electrical and Electronic Equipment directive is aimed at 'e-waste', particularly hazardous materials from computers and related equipment – the dream of a paperless office is attractive from the point of view of tearing down fewer trees but still at present leads to 'cyber pollution'.

The Green Party of Aotearoa New Zealand argues: 'A waste-free society is essential to the well-being of people and the integrity and sustainability of the biosphere. Natural ecosystems are self-sustaining and generate no waste. Humans form part of the ecosystem and, while we access resources from our environment, we have a responsibility to return only those things that can be absorbed without detriment. Waste is not an inevitable part of production and consumption, as it is viewed in the current economic model.'[2]

Land and sea

Agriculture is another important policy area. Greens see the present agribusiness system as one that fuels climate change and other environmental problems, with increasing social inequality as small farmers are eliminated by agribusiness corporations. Small-scale organic agriculture is far more fuel-efficient than the present system, which depends upon large injections of cheap oil, fertilizers and pesticides.

The Green Party of Aotearoa New Zealand notes, for example: 'Farmers are now facing many of the same pressures (escalating land prices and energy costs, high interest and exchange rates, competition from low cost food imports and supermarket downward price pressure) that have resulted in corporate agriculture replacing family farming in Europe and North America. These factors put pressure on farmers to "over-farm" their land in ways that are detrimental to the environment and

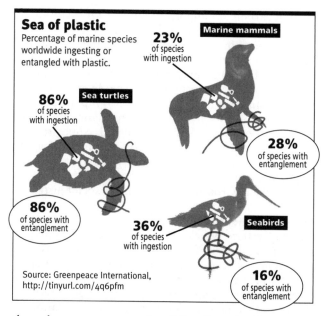

Sea of plastic
Percentage of marine species worldwide ingesting or entangled with plastic.

Marine mammals

23% of species with ingestion

Sea turtles

86% of species with ingestion

28% of species with entanglement

86% of species with entanglement

36% of species with ingestion

Seabirds

16% of species with entanglement

Source: Greenpeace International, http://tinyurl.com/4q6pfm

they also cause personal and family stress.'[3]

Greens tend to oppose the introduction of genetic modification in agriculture, believing that it is potentially dangerous to human health and reduces biodiversity – as well as locking farmers into greater dependency on major agribusiness firms.

The world's seas are heavily polluted and fish stocks are fast declining. Greens have pioneered a range of policies aimed at reversing the decline in the world's oceans. Organic agriculture and an end to factory farming would prevent large quantities of nitrates from washing into the sea, causing algae blooms, which degrade marine ecosystems. Marine conservation areas, which outlaw fishing, are essential if fish stocks are to be allowed to recover. The biggest threat to the world's marine life is acidification from emissions of CO_2, so the range of policies Greens advocate for cutting carbon are important not just for maintaining climate but also for preserving marine life.

This concern for the oceans extends to natural habitats on land. While the notion of wilderness untainted by human presence is a myth, it is possible to maintain habitats so as to preserve biodiversity. Greens have a range of strong conservation policies. The world's rainforests are still home to many indigenous communities who have developed sophisticated management strategies to preserve them. Challenging the assaults on indigenous property is one of the most important policies advocated by Green parties to protect the environment and promote social justice.

Compassion not cruelty

Animal welfare policies flow from the understanding that human beings are part of a larger living network, and compassion for other species tends to be another key characteristic of green politics. Green parties have strong policies on animal welfare, opposing vivisection, the use of animals for cruel forms of entertainment such as bullfighting and fox hunting, factory farming and other forms of abuse. The Green Party of England and Wales, for example, bases its welfare policies on the idea that 'the prevailing assumption that animals can be used for any purpose that benefits humankind is not acceptable in a green society'. And the Party holds to the long-term aim 'to eliminate the wholesale exploitation of other species, foster understanding of our inter-relationship in the web of life and protect and promote natural habitat.'[4]

The Green Party of Canada has courted controversy by opposing seal culling. 'Culling of wild animal populations is generally driven by political rather than scientific motives, and is not supported as a management tool by the vast majority of conservation organizations around the world. Human beings have little understanding of the ways in which species interact, and consequently culling of wild animal populations can often have negative impacts on non-target species and their ecosystems. The Green Party will prohibit the culling of wild animals as a management tool.'[5]

Fair is worth fighting for

Greens have a variety of policies aimed at promoting a fairer society. The major source of inequality is unequal property ownership; Greens are keen advocates of land reform and property redistribution, advocating co-operatives and mutual societies as a means of decentralizing economic control. Income redistribution also plays a key role: Greens generally advocate progressive taxes that take more from those on higher incomes.

A major influence on income and wealth distribution is education. Education is at present increasingly channeled towards providing skills for work and based on a treadmill regime of examinations and tests. Far from simply grading individuals so they can be sorted into careers, education should instead benefit individuals in the broadest sense. Greens believe that equal access to education is an important step towards a more equal society. In consequence, they argue that education should be free, opposing private schools and other forms of selective education. Green voices are raised, therefore, against the privatization of education being urged by the World Trade Organization as part of its General Agreement on Trade in Services (GATS) – they believe education should not be seen as a commodity to be bought and sold but rather as a human right and as part of a lifelong process.

Green parties also tend to support trade union rights, particularly in countries where the weakening of such rights by governments favoring a corporate or neoliberal agenda has led to greater inequality.

Politics for life

Homelessness

Homelessness is rising in many parts of the world, while in other places people squeeze into shanty towns or make do with temporary shelter or squalid, inadequate living conditions. The lack of affordable housing is one factor, and Greens are conscious that expanding the number of homes built has the potential to damage the environment as forests and fields are covered in new dwellings. However, homelessness is a product not just of the number of homes built but of wider market forces. In many Western countries, houses have become a speculative commodity, bought when it is thought that their value will increase as a form of investment. Because of this, many second or third homes bought by individuals lie empty. Green parties promise to discourage multiple home ownership and to act to stop homes lying empty. They aim to prioritize social housing of all kinds, with a view to providing 'affordable rental accommodation to large numbers of people'.[6]

Where new houses are built, Greens would insist on their being low-impact dwellings, built to the highest environmental standards and drawing on sustainable energy sources such as ground heat exchange.

Healthcare

Access to healthcare is another fundamental principle for Green parties worldwide. This issue is particularly vital at present in the US, which spends more per person on healthcare than any other country in the world but where many of the poorest citizens lack any health insurance. The US Green Party strongly supports healthcare reform, advocating a 'single-payer National Health Program to provide free medical and dental care for all, with freedom of choice for consumers among both conventional and alternative healthcare providers, federally financed and controlled by democratically elected local boards'[7]

Greens believe in preventative healthcare, and believe that a green society would also be a happier and healthier one, tackling at root many of the biggest social and environmental sources of ill-health. Greens are also concerned that pharmaceutical companies make huge profits out of their patented drugs and would enable the production of generic drugs that could reach the widest possible number of people in need, particularly in the countries of the Global South.

Many Green parties believe in reforming the current drugs laws, and argue that the use of addictive drugs should be treated as a medical rather than a criminal issue. Greens recognize that illegal drugs, along with legal drugs such as alcohol, cigarettes and many prescription drugs, are addictive and dangerous but are skeptical that prohibition works and see the current 'war on drugs' as evidence of that. Political opponents often use Greens' attitudes towards drug reform as a stick to beat them with, but the position is both practical and ethical. The prohibition of alcohol in the US of the 1930s led to a huge upsurge of violent crime and gang activity, and so too has the prohibition of narcotics.

Grassroots democracy

Green parties in many countries have a range of constitutional policies aimed at making society more democratic. The Scottish Green Party, for example, supported a constitutional convention that reformed the political system. During the 1980s and 1990s, Scottish people consistently voted against the UK's governing Conservative Party but had no say in the way that the Conservatives were running Scotland. More and more Scottish citizens felt they were excluded from the political system. Independent campaigners and a range of Scottish political parties campaigned for a new constitution. This was introduced in response to massive grassroots pressure after the Labour Party finally came to power and, in 1999, a Scottish Parliament with strong powers came into being, the first time Scotland had had a parliament since 1707.

Green parties and human rights

Unsurprisingly, Greens have strong human rights policies. In the US, the Green Party has been critical of what it sees as an assault on human rights by the federal government, especially as part of George W Bush's 'war on terrorism'. It has observed: 'The USA Patriot Act, passed with full bipartisan support in Congress rapidly after 9/11 with only two hours of hearings, allows government to pry into library withdrawals, charge card records, medical and financial data, e-mail, conduct a wire-tap under a general warrant, declare someone a "terrorist" for political dissent and search his or her home without a warrant.'[1]

Greens generally believe in reducing immigration controls and note that migration is primarily a product of an unequal world. They stress the value of cultural diversity and the raised awareness of other cultures that arise from migration. The Green Party of England and Wales considers: 'The existing economic order and colonialism have both been major causes of migration through direct and indirect violence, disruption of traditional economies, the use of migrants as cheap labor, uneven patterns of development and global division of labor... We are aware that, in the 21st century, there is likely to be mass migration of people escaping from the consequences of global warming, environmental degradation, resource shortage and population increase.'[2]

Greens also have strong policies supporting sexual diversity and LGBT (Lesbian, Gay, Bisexual and Transsexual) rights, including gay marriage. The US Green Party summarizes its attitude to rights and liberties in this way: 'All persons should have the rights and opportunity to benefit equally from the resources afforded us by society and the environment. We must consciously confront in ourselves, our organizations, and society at large, barriers such as racism and class oppression, sexism and homophobia, ageism and disability, which act to deny fair treatment and equal justice under the law.'[3]

After a long battle, the Green Party of Aotearoa New Zealand managed to make anti-smacking legislation part of New Zealand law and all Green parties tend to have policies aimed at safeguarding children's rights and opposing violent forms of punishment by parents and guardians. ∎

1 http://tinyurl.com/ydnq6mw
2 http://policy.greenparty.org.uk/mfss/mfssmg.html
3 www.gp.org/position/st_2006_04_26.shtml

Proportional representation was introduced for the parliament and for local elections in Scotland. In the US, Canada and the rest of the UK, the Greens are largely excluded thanks to the first-past-the-post electoral system, which acts to the benefit of the large, established political parties. Much of the strength of Green parties in Europe outside the UK has been facilitated by voting systems based on proportional representation.

The US Greens believe that, despite the mainstream rhetoric about their country being the homeland of democracy, only major reforms can make the US truly democratic. They point to the vast amounts of money involved in US politics, to the complex rules that make it difficult for parties other than the Democrats or Republicans to contest many elections and to the existence of the Senate as the upper house in Congress. The Green Party of Aotearoa New Zealand is also anxious about the influence of corporate interests on politics and believes in limiting donations to political parties.

Greens universally fear that globalization based on a neoliberal agenda will take power further away from local people, with more and more decisions being shaped by the needs of corporations. In this respect, Greens tend to have contradictory responses to the European Union. Some Greens are very hostile to the European Union, seeing it as an unreformable force that centralizes power and is driven by corruption. For example, the Danish Green Party was expelled from the European Green Party group for supporting an anti-EU group in European elections. The Green Party of England and Wales is critical of a single currency, which it believes works for the benefit of corporate interests, and is worried that the EU is far from democratic. The Swedish Green Party is also critical of the European Union but does not seek Swedish withdrawal. On the other hand, most European Green parties believe that the EU has the potential to act as a counterweight to the worst features of globalization and that it provides a means of introducing stronger environmental and social policies.

Green demands for democracy involve support for a more radical decentralization of power to give people a direct say in decision-making. The US Greens advocate what amounts to sweeping changes in the US system to give power back to people. The Green Party of Canada also believes in sweeping democratic reform: 'Canadian democracy would benefit by reducing the financial barriers to running for political office, lowering the voter age to encourage more youth participation, and changing to a voting system that more fairly translates people's votes into representation in parliament.'[8]

Green peace

Green parties are, of course, strong advocates of peace. Green parties believe in abolishing all nuclear weapons and many of their members, particularly in France and Germany, came out of the anti-nuclear peace movements. During the 1980s, Green parties were very active in pressing for nuclear disarmament in the face of rising tension between the US and the Soviet bloc. Anti-nuclear weapons policies remain important today, even though the huge threat presented by nuclear weapons is often forgotten.

Greens strongly oppose chemical and biological warfare. They tend to believe in reducing the power of armed forces and in cutting military spending to the bone. In Jean Luc Godard's *La Chinoise*, one of the characters remarks that the army should have to go fundraising to find the money to fight wars, instead of using public money that could be spent on schools and hospitals. This is an attitude that would ring bells in most Green gatherings, where the arms trade would be another natural target.

Greens take a firmly anti-imperialist line and believe that, where military intervention is necessary, it should be headed by the United Nations. They thus tend to be critical of the wars currently being fought in Afghanistan and Iraq, which they see as being tainted by the leadership of imperial powers like the US and Britain. Many Greens stop short of pacifism, and have been sympathetic to liberation movements such as the ANC in South Africa. They believe, however, that nonviolent resistance is normally the most appropriate course and feel that the best way to prevent war is to address the underlying injustices and insecurities that lie behind it.

The Green Party of England and Wales sums up the Green view of conflict in this way: 'Warfare in the context of present offensive weapon systems, nuclear or non-nuclear, is so dangerous that it cannot be regarded as a sane instrument of policy. Common security measures seek to build trust and co-operation, to prevent destructive conflict, to build a just local and global society based upon fairness.'[9]

Green parties recognize, for example, that the current conflict in the Middle East will only be resolved if Palestinians feel they have been given appropriate recognition and justice. The US Greens are critical of the support given by the US government to Israel but conscious that, for peace to be achieved, not only must Palestinians be treated with justice but also both sides must feel secure. The Party advocates a Truth and Reconciliation Commission like that which operated in South Africa as a tool for achieving mutual trust and enduring peace.

Aid and development

Green internationalism is based on pursuing peace and social justice across the globe. Because of this, Greens are critical of much present policy on 'development'. Policies aimed at reducing global poverty are often built on false assumptions. The Washington Consensus that has governed the policies of the International Monetary Fund, World Bank and World Trade Organization is based on the removal of barriers to the market, increased free trade, free movement of currency, privatization and a reduction in state spending. Such policies have accelerated inequality and undermined sustainable development.

Green parties tend to support higher levels of development aid. The Green Party of Canada, for instance, is among those committed to meeting the UN target of 0.7 per cent of the country's GDP being devoted to overseas aid. 'This level of funding,' it says, 'is essential to meet the most basic of goals: to make poverty history, cure disease, foster democracy, and support ecologically sustainable economies. This will make the world a better and safer place for everyone.'[10] Most Green parties consider development aid to be only part of the picture, however, believing that international policy should be based on the pursuit of justice and democracy rather than the interests of transnational corporations and financiers.

This has been the most cursory of whistlestop tours around green policies. However, it is clear even from this rather brief survey that Green parties have extensive policies ranging across all areas of the political agenda. These policies flow from core commitments not only to the environment but also to social justice, peace and grassroots democracy. It is all very well, however, taking up policy positions from the sidelines. The goal of actually implementing such policies means that Greens have to consider questions of power and strategy. Greens can clearly not afford to wait for the day when they win elections and form governments in their own right but need to press for change in the here and now. The last chapter examines green approaches to power, change, tactics and strategy – how greens are currently engaged in remaking our world.

1 http://policy.greenparty.org.uk/mfss/men.html
2 www.greens.org.nz/node/17458
3 www.greens.org.nz/policy/agriculture
4 http://policy.greenparty.org.uk/mfss/mar.html
5 www.greenparty.ca/en/policy/documents/animal_protection
6 www.greens.org.nz/node/19598
7 www.greenparty.org/Platform.php
8 www.greenparty.ca/en/policy/visiongreen/partsix
9 policy.greenparty.org.uk/mfss/mfsspd.html
10 www.greenparty.ca/en/policy/visiongreen/partfive

6 Strategies for survival

The green movement has come a long way since its early days of optimistic idealism and student revolt. It has seen Green parties share power in governments – and wrestle with compromise along the way. But the movement is multi-faceted, embracing direct action and lifestyle change, 'green business' and indigenous campaigners. Humanity's future may rest on its ultimate success – and new developments in Latin America offer hope.

GREEN POLITICS IS, like all politics, about power, change and strategy. Given the urgency of the ecological crisis, the strategic question is more vital for greens than for followers of other ideologies. When Lenin wrote 'What is to be done?' he did not feel that failure to a make a revolution in Czarist Russia would led to devastating environmental destruction. When Gandhi worked to end British rule in India he was not working against the clock to stop climate change. Green political strategy is important given the reality of climate change and the genuine fear that we are very close to a tipping point beyond which calamitous destruction will be inevitable. The methods that have been used by greens to create the change needed are varied. Elections, nonviolent direct action, work in NGOs, lifestyle change and cultural strategies: all these have been employed in the attempt to create the necessary transformation. Green party politics is just one arrow to this bow, and even Green parties have a wider focus than simply fighting and winning elections.

Green parties were created amid a situation of contradictory political pressures, which pulled them in different strategic directions. One assumption that was abroad at the time of their formation was that the ecological problems were so obvious and so important that green politics was about little more than unveiling a plan that would be put into action – either by existing politicians, or by a new party which would win a majority of votes when citizens realized how dangerous the situation was and how urgent was the need for change.

In the UK, the Green Party's origins can be traced back to the publication of *Blueprint for Survival*. This document suggested that a manifesto of ecological demands should be put to existing politicians and that, if they ignored such a manifesto, an ecological party should be created. Once it had won governmental power, the party would instigate an ecological path for the country. 'It must now give rise to a national movement to act at a national level, and if need be to assume political status and contest the next general election. It is hoped that such an example will be emulated in other countries, thereby giving rise to an international movement.'[1]

Essentially it was assumed that government, business, trade unions and the public would listen to the authors of *Blueprint* and put into practice an ecological plan. *Blueprint* contains a flow chart illustrating the creation of an ecological and decentralist Britain, which starts in 1975 and goes up to 2075. The assumption was that the powers-that-be would roll out such a plan and put it into action. If they didn't, a Movement for Survival would form a political party that would contest all Westminster parliamentary seats, elect MPs, form a government and introduce a new ecological Britain over a period of a hundred years. The implicit assumption was that either the necessary changes would be introduced by the existing political establishment or, if they proved unwilling, a new green establishment would swiftly take over. *Blueprint* was very much a top-down vision of how to get to a bottom-up society.

A product of revolt

Green politics is, however, as much a product of revolt as of the musings of a would-be ecological élite. It is to some extent the political expression of the student revolts against the Vietnam War, the French year of protest in 1968 and, above all, the German social movements of the 1960s and 1970s. Interestingly, at the outset, some political ecologists – notably Edward Goldsmith – assumed that they were very much part of the establishment, while others were at the cutting edge of movements to overturn the establishment through disruptive protest. Rudi Dutschke, the German student leader, argued for 'a long march through the institutions'. Indeed the German Greens originated as an 'anti-party party', a wing of social movements, which aimed to turn Dutshcke's vision into a reality.

By the year 2000, however, Green parties had evolved into something of a compromise between these two views. Neither the élitist nor the anarchist sentiments have quite been realized. The assumption that greens would simply step into power was totally unrealistic, but while the anti-authoritarian student protest movements melted away, Green parties have managed to have candidates elected to parliament in many parts of the world and to introduce reforms. Especially in western Europe, greens have gained a stable position as minority political parties, gaining between 5 and 10 per cent of the vote, often participating in governing coalitions and creating a measure of environmental change.

In Germany, the Greens went into government with the Social Democrats. Solid gains included transforming Germany into the world center for renewable energy and beginning to phase out nuclear power. Green left coalitions have also occurred in Belgium, France, Sweden and Austria. In Iceland in 2009, after the collapse of the free-market Independence Party, the Green Left Movement went into coalition government. More controversial coalitions have also been created with parties of the Right – in Ireland, for example, the Green Party went into government with the center-right Fianna Fail Party in 2007. In 2009, the German Greens joined a so-called Jamaica coalition of green, black and yellow in Saarland, with the Christian Democrats and Free Democrats.

None of these coalitions have realized the most radical green policies outlined earlier. Practical gains have been made but there have been a number of often dramatic and surprising compromises. In Iceland, for instance, the coalition government has continued to allow whaling. In Germany, meanwhile, despite the Greens being seen as the political expression of the peace movement, the coalition government kept the country in NATO. Germany's participation in wars in Serbia and Afghanistan proved even more controversial. Shockingly, in Ireland, the government has pressed on with plans to build a motorway close to the previously protected prehistoric landscape of Tara.

The idea that a green society could easily be legislated into being has come to seem unrealistic but the opposing notion that Green parties would disappear quickly has not occurred either. With the increasing awareness of the environmental crisis, Green parties are likely to grow and become politically more influential. The idea that they will win power in their own right within the few short years necessary to create change seems unlikely. The Green Party of England and Wales, for example, is growing but it is likely to be some time before it gets close to governmental power. Unfortunately, in terms of combating climate change, time must be measured in years or even months rather than in decades.

One alternative has been to try to 'green' larger and more established political parties. In the UK, for example, the Socialist Environment Resources Association has over many years tried to green the Labour Party, while Edward Goldsmith's nephew Zac

Strategies for survival

Goldsmith has tried to green the Conservative Party and is likely to be a Member of Parliament by the time you read this chapter. The idea of taking over a traditional party and turning it green seems rather more attractive than slogging on the doorsteps to put an actual Green party in government. This superficially appealing strategy has, however, not produced major success so far. Despite some green noises, traditional political parties have generally moved to the free-market right over recent decades. Certainly none of them have been willing to question economic growth or to base their politics on fundamental green principles. It can also be argued that competition for votes from real Green parties is likely to be an easier and more efficient route to influencing other political parties than subverting them from within.

Direct action

Another path to green political change has occurred through nonviolent direct action. Groups like Earth First!, Reclaim the Streets and Groen Front have used direct action to try to halt environmentally destructive projects and to promote ecological change. Despite coming from a deep ecology perspective, they have engaged with the broad scope of green politics, fighting for asylum rights, working with trade unionists and calling for social change. To some extent, these groups reflect disillusionment with Green party strategies. The evolution of student radicals like Danny Cohn-Bendit and Joschka Fischer into suited parliamentarians has led to a backlash.

Supporters of green direct action networks argue that corporate power uses the state to maintain its destructive goals, so that green political parties will either be marginalized or become compromised, even if elected. Direct action, they argue, can halt ecological destruction and prefigure a direct democracy where communities rather than corporations can work for change. Reclaim the Streets (RTS) has argued that: 'Voting is a weapon of government to delude people into thinking that they have a say in how the country is run, to reinforce their passive role and encourage them to leave the "politics" to the specialists. The alternative message that RTS were pushing was one of empowerment – for people to participate in direct action, not only in the political arena, but also in all aspects of their lives. It was an attempt to dissuade people from the belief that we can change things by working within the system, when it is the system itself that we must destroy if we are to have any meaningful and lasting change.'[2]

Rudolf Bahro resigned from the German Greens in the 1980s, arguing that environmental reforms introduced by the party would actually make it more difficult to change society. He suggested that pollution controls and other forms of regulation were like cleaning the dragon's breath – superficial changes that would make it easier for the system of destruction to keep on growing. His critics, in turn, have argued that creating some change is better than preaching from the sidelines a message of radicalism that has no effect at all on prevailing power structures and policies. Green direct action has probably been just as effective as Green party electoral politics – if not more so. It too, however, has been more influential in achieving small reforms than in bringing about a wider transformation of society. Also, paradoxically, green direct action has grown along with Green parties.

The climate camp movement in the UK seems to have been particularly effective. Mobilizing thousands of individuals, it has, at least temporarily, shut down coal-burning power stations and drawn attention to the chaos likely to be caused by climate change. Groups like Plane Stupid have embarrassed politicians and disrupted flights. But direct action alone may not be enough to change the system. Disrupting symptoms of the system driving environmental damage may be possible but this is not the same as creating a new and sustainable society.

Changing lifestyle

Green politics has also used lifestyle strategies, promoting personal change and practical alternatives.

Plane Stupid: why take direct action?

People often ask me why Plane Stupid takes direct action instead of lobbying our MPs like good boys and girls. Once I've finished supergluing myself to their flight to Tuscany, I tell them that it's complicated and that everyone has their own reasons for taking action. They're usually not satisfied with that, so in the long hours before the cops show up, I explain the four main arguments.

DIRECT ACTION WORKS. History has shown us that when there is a need for radical social change, asking those in power nicely to relinquish some control doesn't get us very far. There would be no trade unions without the Tolpuddle martyrs, nor marches and rallies without Peterloo.

Women wouldn't be voting without the suffragettes. Mandela would still be in jail if it wasn't for direct action against apartheid. India would still be a British colony and Rosa Parks' grandkids would be at the back of the bus. Britain would be covered in new motorways and GM crops. Even if you don't agree with our methods and aims you can't really deny that the world is a better place because of people taking direct action.

DIRECT ACTION GETS STRAIGHT TO THE POINT. Sometimes you're left with no choice but to take action. Developers want to bulldoze your house to build an airport. Your family will be on the streets because the banks won't re-mortgage your house. An old lady is getting mugged in front of you at the bus stop. Your boss plans to fire loads of staff to protect his bonus. The biosphere is collapsing because industrial growth keeps consuming our dwindling resources.

These aren't times to write your MP a nice letter asking whether he saw the petition you signed. There's no time to go to the police or the courts (even if you could afford it), and there's no betting they'd support you if you did. These are all times to take action with friends, co-workers, neighbors and complete strangers. When systems fail you, don't fail yourself.

REPRESENTATIVE DEMOCRACY IS FAILING. These days we don't trust politicians to fill in expenses forms, so why should we trust them with the most important aspects of our lives? Businesses spend millions

---

Participation in nonviolent direct action can be costly in terms of time and the risk of prosecution or even imprisonment. Equally, with power moving away from parliaments in a globalized world and electoral politics often appearing empty, the idea of personal change may seem more attractive.

Like any other strategy, however, personal change has

every year on fancy dinners and seats on the board, which gives them more of a say in how our country is run than we have. Voting once every four years is not enough: we need to regain control over our own food supplies, our jobs, our shelter, our transport systems and our futures.

Climate change isn't an accident: it's happening because people in power profit from it – often the very governments and businesses offering us a way out. We can't afford to defer power to governments we didn't vote for and the corporations we didn't ask for. We need to build direct ways of taking back control of our lives and an ethic of direct action can be a part of this.

DIRECT ACTION TAKES RESPONSIBILITY FOR THE WORLD WE SEE AROUND US. Dealing with climate change is our collective responsibility. We can't leave it up to the powerful to solve it: they got us into this mess in the first place, and the money they made doing so will make sure they're the last ones to be affected by it.

Corporate and market-based solutions, like carbon trading and green taxation, are as much about keeping those in power where they are as tackling rising greenhouse gas emissions. Direct action is about recognizing the false solutions and building real alternatives; about being the change we want to see in the world.

For many, direct action is a preferred way of doing things through which we can take both responsibility and control: two sides of the same coin which we unwisely let fall into another's purse when we allow the powerful to dictate the terms of business.

We passionately believe in direct action but we also believe that it must be justifiable and this is why we complement it with horizontal organization, direct democracy and consensus to decide what action to take.

So while we're sorry that your flight was delayed because of what we did, we had to take action. I'll get all worthy and quote Martin Luther King here: 'Our lives begin to end the day we become silent about things that matter.' See you on the barricades? ∎

Posted by 'Barry' for Plane Stupid on 18 June 2009, www.planestupid.com/blogs/2009/06/18/plane-stupid-explains-why-take-direct-action both strengths and weaknesses. On the plus side, if a large number of individuals reduce their impact on the environment, this will help slow ecological catastrophe, while if green lifestyles prove attractive enough and snowball, this could eventually lead to a new ecological civilization. And it is certainly true that whatever strategy greens adopt, personal lifestyles based on wasteful and polluting over-consumption are hypocritical for those advocating an environmentally sustainable future. Lifestyle change is also attractive because it does not require the election of Members of Parliament or sudden revolutionary change – it is something to which we can all contribute now.

However, while lifestyle change appears to be an appealing option, even this is not without problems. Perhaps most significantly, it can distract from the wider structural change needed in society to make green goals realistic. In many parts of the world, where the economy is so centralized that journeys to work are relatively long but where public transport is poor or nonexistent, people are dependent on car use. Living outside the great car economy may be impossible for many people. For a variety of reasons, including restrictive planning regulations, structures put into place by politicians may lock us into high carbon use. Reducing car use, eating less meat and improving energy efficiency are all necessary, but without wider political change they will be insufficient. Lifestyle politics may even distract from the more radical changes needed and absorb individuals in time-consuming activities that induce guilt faster than they create real transformation. Personal change certainly plays a part in green politics but individualist action can often obscure the need for structural transformation and political engagement.

A new movement for Transition Towns tries to overcome the limits of personal action and political activity by engaging whole communities so as to introduce the changes necessary to move to a low-carbon future. The Transition Towns movement is currently growing fast, especially in Britain, New Zealand/Aotearoa and Australia. It works to design a step-by-step plan to wean particular towns from dependence on fossil fuels. Initially developed in Kinsale, Ireland, the first step is usually to call a public meeting to enthuse local people and try to get local politicians on board. By trying to change structures, the movement has a more powerful effect than individual lifestyle change but it avoids the need for party politics or militant direct action. It is assumed that Transition Towns will draw in people who may be disillusioned with party politics. Rob Hopkins, who helped develop the Transition Town concept and works tirelessly to promote it, practices permaculture and seeks to apply many of the permaculture principles to town development. There is a great emphasis in the Transition Town strategy on creating local economies – one tactic, for example, is to promote local currencies that will help build up local businesses, rather than seeing supermarkets take over.

The movement begins by raising awareness of issues such as climate change and peak oil at a local level, so as to nurture a commitment to change. Bridges are then built to existing groups in the community, especially those committed to environmental change, links are forged with local government, and groups are formed to plan for change in key areas such as food, energy, transport, health and economics. The next step is to develop an 'Energy Descent Action Plan' which can be implemented over a 15-to-20-year timescale. The movement sees transition as inevitable but wishes to make it as attractive and painless as possible.

This strategy certainly seems much more realistic than the *Blueprint for Survival* plan for top-down change over many decades by green governments. Change that is instigated by local communities is more likely to gain support, and built into the transition strategy is the opportunity for flexibility and creative input from local communities. Transition towns utilize a peer-to-peer strategy, similar to software design – different people can input and it makes use of diverse skills. As with wikis and free software projects, local communities do not need to start from scratch but can utilize experience from all over the world.

The closest to a real-world example of a transition town strategy taking shape has been in Cuba, where, as we noted, permaculture and other low-energy solutions have been introduced on a large scale. The success of the Cuban example has not been down to a specific transition strategy but rather was forced by the sudden removal of cheap oil. Supporters of the Transition Town concept argue that the era of cheap oil is over for the entire world, and that their approach will therefore grow very fast. Critics argue that only strong grassroots communities can introduce the necessary changes and that the power of community in Cuba allowed fast change to occur. Community building is one major challenge for the Transition Town movement. It is easy to be skeptical and imagine that the concept will appeal most to those already involved in the green movement. For all its novel features, similar projects for grassroots change such as local exchange and trading schemes (LETS) have been around for several decades without creating a green revolution.

Ted Trainer, the radical Australian ecologist, has undertaken a sympathetic criticism of the Transition Towns concept. He argues that 'there is the danger that it will only be a Not-In-My-Backyard phenomenon, that it will be about towns trying to insulate themselves from the coming time of scarcities and troubles. This is a quite different goal from working to replace consumer-capitalist society. It is not much good if your town bakes its own bread or even generates much of its own electricity, while it goes on importing hardware and appliances produced in China and taking holidays abroad. It will still indirectly be using considerable amounts of coal and oil in the goods it imports.'[3] He also believes that not enough practical detail as to how communities will make the transition has been discussed. The concept of transition towns tends, he feels, to ignore the big structures of global economics and national governments that negatively shape energy use and environmental impact at present.

Green business

Another strategy to create change has been via green business projects. In the late 1980s, Julia Hailes and John Elkington published two books, *The Green Consumer Guide* and *The Green Capitalists*. Both enjoyed huge sales and had a major impact. The US environmentalists Paul Hawken and Amory Lovins have developed the concept of 'Natural Capitalism'. According to their argument: if businesses are so powerful and so influential, then why not use them to create environmental change?[4] Businesses will inevitably have to go green, it has been argued, because rising fuel costs will force them to become more efficient. Increasingly, it can also be argued that we have more power as consumers than as voters. In a more recent book, *Cannibals with Forks: The Triple Bottom Line of 21st Century Business*, Elkington has argued that, if they are to prosper, modern businesses need to account for social and environmental factors as well as financial success. More recently, Jonathon Porritt, perhaps the best-known member of the green movement in Britain, has suggested that the 'natural capitalism' concept can be use to create 'capitalism as if the world mattered'.[5]

Again, while genuine attempts by business to reduce

their environmental impact are to be welcomed, this strategy also involves severe risks. It avoids much of the wider green agenda: environmentally friendly businesses may not, for example, promote better pay and working conditions to fulfill the green demand for social justice. The business world is increasingly globalized, with powerful monopolies dominating much of the economy, and the decentralist vision is challenged by such business growth. There are, however, some interesting examples of green businesses which do positive work. The British cosmetics firm Lush has, for instance, banned palm oil, which often comes from plantations on cleared rainforest land, and

Will capitalism survive climate change?

In contrast to the Northern élites' strategy of trying to decouple growth from energy use, a progressive comprehensive climate strategy in both the North and the South must be to reduce growth and energy use while raising the quality of life of the broad masses of people. Among other things, this will mean placing economic justice and equality at the center of the new paradigm.

The transition must be one not only from a fossil-fuel-based economy but also from an overconsumption-driven economy. The end-goal must be adoption of a low-consumption, low-growth, high-equity development model that results in an improvement in people's welfare, a better quality of life for all, and greater democratic control of production.

It is unlikely that the élites of the North and the South will agree to such a comprehensive response. The farthest they are likely to go is for technofixes and a market-based cap-and-trade system. Growth will be sacrosanct, as will the system of global capitalism.

Yet, confronted with the Apocalypse, humanity cannot self-destruct. It may be a difficult road, but we can be sure that the vast majority will not commit social and ecological suicide to enable the minority to preserve their privileges. However it is achieved, a thorough reorganization of production, consumption and distribution will be the end result of humanity's response to the climate emergency and the broader environmental crisis. ∎

Excerpted from Walden Bello, 'Will capitalism survive climate change?' Transnational Institute, 1 Apr 2008, www.tni.org/detail_page.phtml?act_id=18103

donates to Plane Stupid, the direct-action movement against airport expansion.

While green business has grown as a concept, with more and more goods marketed as green, it has not resulted in the slowing of the threats to the planet. Sales of organic food have risen sharply with rising public concern over the environmental and health effects of agribusiness, yet organic can seem like just another profitable form of niche marketing. Organic consumers can be charged more but most of the world's food continues to be produced in fossil-fuel-dependent and ecologically damaging ways. Markets don't automatically lead to conservation – for example, as the price of oil rises the pressure on fragile ecosystems will rise too, as there is then a greater incentive to destroy them so as to extract profitable fossil fuels. The destructive growth of biofuels is another good example of this process.

A real danger is that green business is more about superficial, spray-on green marketing than about truly greening production. Oil companies often sponsor environmental groups, local conservation efforts and tree planting to green their image and thereby reduce the pressure on them to make a serious move into renewable energy production. Businesses tend to make more money when consumers consume more. The environmental crisis requires us to consume less, which seems to contradict the green business ethic. Likewise, ethical investment, including green investment, while growing, is still small as a proportion of the total market and often is far less green than it at first appears. Green politics is about alternatives to growth and as such challenge many business interests.

Green trade unions
Yet another approach has been to promote green trade unionism. While it is often argued that trade unionists, like many businesspeople, will oppose

green politics because reduced growth will lead to fewer jobs, the number of examples of environmental campaigns won by trade union action is surprisingly large. In any event, there are some areas of the economy that would of course expand in the transition to a post-fossil-fuel future. The Green New Deal, which is based on expanding public transport, renewable energy production and insulation, would certainly create jobs.

Other sectors of the economy will also need to be transformed, since car manufacture, weapons building and pesticide production, for example, will either be discontinued or be radically changed. Plans to give workers control over this kind of transformation of production will be vital to achieving such change and making it acceptable.

Currently trade unionists in the UK are developing plans to convert Trident missile production into alternative products. In the 1970s, at Lucas Aerospace, workers led by the shop steward Mike Cooley developed a detailed plan for such conversion. At the time, the company mainly produced military equipment for NATO and jobs were under threat. The Lucas workers researched a range of socially useful and environmentally friendly goods that they could produce instead of military equipment using their existing manufacturing plant and skills. The workers came up with detailed plans to build kidney machines, renewable-energy equipment, road-rail buses and other useful products. Sadly, the workers' plan was not put into action but it illustrates the imaginative capacity and willingness to change of trade unionists.

Workers are also some of the people affected most by pollution. Pollution at work is a health and safety issue that has the potential to kill; trade unionists have a self-interested desire to work in safe and clean conditions. There are even examples of green strikes and other forms of industrial action. In the 1970s, the Australian Building Workers Union undertook 'green bans' – this meant they refused to work where construction led to damage to conservation zones. During the 1980s, workers in Britain's National Union of Seamen (now part of the Rail Maritime and Transport union) refused to dump low-level nuclear waste at sea, and as a result of this such dumping was discontinued. In the US, the late Judi Bari, a member of Earth First!, established links with logging unions to conserve forests. In Britain today a trade union climate change campaign is currently working on an ambitious plan to create jobs in the transition to a low-carbon future.

Strategies involving economic change are likely to be vital. It is very difficult to see how support for a greener economy can be achieved without gaining trade union support. Green strategies also involve promoting economic localization. The creation of democratically owned and run businesses is also likely to be of importance, since corporations that operate globally and have a legal requirement to maximize profit are unlikely to support necessary change. Indeed, co-operative and mutual businesses are growing fast – it was notable amid the financial meltdown of 2008-09 that these had tended to avoid the riskier and more irresponsible kinds of speculation that had brought about the crisis.

Other greens put their energy into pressure-group activity, confident that NGOs will have an important role in developing new policies, influencing government and business, and researching the practical changes necessary. There are numerous and increasingly effective NGOs in the field, but these tend to stress environmental demands rather than the wider range of concerns in green politics. They also have to compete for the ear of government with corporate groups who seek to water down environmental legislation and use green concerns as a way of expanding profit rather than protecting life.

Transforming the culture

Finally, there are strategies based on green cultural change. The deep politics behind both our voting decisions and the assumptions of planners and policy-makers is based on fundamental and often unconscious beliefs about our relationship to the rest of nature and to each other.

The need for cultural change may be even more fundamental than that for political or economic transformation. As Ted Trainer notes: 'More problematic than the need for a radically different economy would be the acceptance of some values which clash with the Western tradition, notably the present commitments to competition, individualism and acquisitiveness, and the conception of progress.'[6] Many deep ecologists feel that personal spiritual change is the most important step to a greener world. Indigenous people, in many parts of world, have maintained environmental diversity, at least in part because their economic and social activity is underpinned by an Earth ethic that respects the rest of nature.

Environmental stewardship is found in a variety of religions. Religious notions have been used to advance practical conservation. Fishing communities in Zanzibar have, for example, changed their fishing strategies to conserve the local environment in line with stewardship notions in the Qur'an: 'We are the guardians of God's creation. He asks us to protect what he created and we can do this by looking after the environment.'[7]

There are obvious limits to this approach of promoting green religion in a world that is both diverse and increasingly secular. Some religions have dubious attitudes towards women and sexual minorities that greens would not endorse. In theory, most religions promote values shared with the green movement, such as social justice and peace, but in practice they have often embraced war and injustice.

The idea of sending out green missionaries from various world faiths seems a little naive. It does, however, illustrate that green politics needs to become part of culture. Fighting elections, using direct action or creating Transition Towns: none of these strategies are likely to achieve their ultimate goals if they are not reinforced by cultural change. Green cultural change should be part of all green strategies. The sociologist Alberto Melucci argued that, when social movements are their most successful, they develop new social codes, which they transmit to the rest of society.[8] Social movements can move ideas from the margin to the mainstream that were previously unthought of or unthinkably radical. The notion of social codes is similar to the idea of a meme (a set of concepts that can be communicated to others). This means that greens fighting elections should not simply frame their message so as to maximize votes in the short term, however urgent the situation. To succeed, green politics must accelerate the adoption of new attitudes to the environment and economics.

Only by promoting cultural change will political, social and economic structures be transformed – it is not the only means of achieving change but it is an essential element. Achieving such cultural change is arguably even more challenging than facing up to vested economic interests, winning elections or successfully undertaking nonviolent direct action.

Green politics needs to overcome huge vested interests to develop an ecological society and part of the process will involve deep-seated cultural change. It is easy to dismiss many green strategies as hopelessly reformist and to see Green parties and pressure groups as the likely victims of incorporation into a destructive system that seduces radicals. Sometimes it seems that individual campaigners are inevitably drawn into bed with polluting corporate interests. Yet it is as dangerous to do nothing while retaining impotent political purity as it is to be sucked into the system. How the green movement can develop political alternatives that create change without being marginalized or corrupted is the challenge that will shape both the future of green politics and the entire planet. It is a challenge that needs to be developed very quickly indeed if we are to have a future.

Hope from Latin America

William Morris, the green socialist and novelist, over a century ago noted in his poem *A dream of John Ball*: 'how men fight and lose the battle, and the thing that they fought for comes about in spite of their defeat, and when it comes turns out not to be what they meant, and other men have to fight for what they meant under another name'.[9] Perhaps if he had included women as well, this thought might express the paradox of green politics in the 21st century.

Some would argue that many Green parties and environmental NGOs have become hopelessly reformist and compromised. Even though it is possible to challenge this view and this book focuses on the many achievements of Green parties and their commitments to radical policies, there is some sense in the observation borrowed from William Morris.

In particular, the campaign for climate justice – for effective policies that cut carbon and other greenhouse gases while increasing equality – seems no longer to be spearheaded by Green parties or even by the more radical green protest movements at the grassroots. The Latin American Left, and most specifically the indigenous part, seems to be in the vanguard of a political struggle for the green goals of ecology, social justice, peace and grassroots democracy.

In Peru, the government of Alan Garcia has been keen to relax laws protecting indigenous control of the Amazon so as to attract foreign investment. Much of the rainforest – as well as large parts of Peru outside of the rainforests – is controlled by indigenous people, who have land rights systems that give free access to land. The indigenous believe that oil exploration and other forms of 'development' would bring them little economic benefit. The profits made by companies would go abroad and locals would not gain jobs in oil or similar industries. In essence, their land – their most vital economic resource – would be taken and they would have no means of subsistence.

Peru's indigenous peoples are skeptical that economic development would make them prosper in conventional terms. To a large extent such a sentiment is common in Latin America, with a resource-based economy benefiting relatively small élites and doing little for the mass of the population. In countries like Bolivia and Venezuela, new leaders representing the poor have been elected on promises to use resource revenue to benefit the wider population and to nationalize oil and gas production.

The indigenous peoples in Peru have varied social systems and outlooks. In 2008 and 2009, over 50 different indigenous groups linked together and took nonviolent direct action to defend their land. In both years, their organization – AIDESEP, the inter-cultural network of the Peruvian Amazon – blocked roads and river traffic to force the government to recognize their rights to live in the rainforest and to prevent its destruction by corporations.

Their fight in Peru has so far succeeded, but on World Environment Day, 5 June 2009, many indigenous protestors were killed by Peru's paramilitary police. Shockingly, most governments around the world ignored this act of violent repression and most environmentalists are unaware of the struggles of

Strategies for survival

AIDESEP and similar organizations.

The indigenous in Peru have been inspired by an ecological ethos, which means that, while they might not use the term, they are very much part of green politics. Right across Latin America, indigenous people have been mobilizing. They also have links with indigenous groups in Canada and the US. They are at the frontline of battling climate change and other ecological ills, although their contribution is often forgotten.

The indigenous peoples have provided an interesting contribution to debates around notions of growth, development and prosperity. They don't reject modernity – after all, I communicate with them and know about their work via emails and websites – but they certainly want development that respects nature and works to promote social equality.

From Copenhagen to Cochabamba

In December 2009, at the Copenhagen conference on climate change, this Latin American frontline role for Latin Americans was underlined. Copenhagen was the latest stage in a series of global conferences set up to forge international agreements to limit CO_2 and other greenhouse gases. For many people, the conference was a devastating failure – no binding agreement was reached and the guidelines put forward at the instigation of US President Obama seemed far too weak to have any real effect. Heavy-handed policing led to many demonstrators and even some official delegates being attacked on the streets. There has also been an upsurge in climate skepticism, with public concern or even belief in the reality of human-induced climate change falling rapidly in Western. Even if there had been a strong outcome, the framework discussed at conferences such as Copenhagen is based on carbon trading, which, as we have seen in Chapter 2, is flawed and unjust.

An Indigenous view of the climate crisis

From 20-24 April 2009, Indigenous representatives from the Arctic, North America, Asia, Pacific, Latin America, Africa, Caribbean and Russia met in Anchorage, Alaska for the Indigenous Peoples' Global Summit on Climate Change. We thank the Ahtna and the Dena'ina Athabascan Peoples in whose lands we gathered.

We express our solidarity as Indigenous Peoples living in areas that are the most vulnerable to the impacts and root causes of climate change. We reaffirm the unbreakable and sacred connection between land, air, water, oceans, forests, sea ice, plants, animals and our human communities as the material and spiritual basis for our existence.

We are deeply alarmed by the accelerating climate devastation brought about by unsustainable development. We are experiencing profound and disproportionate adverse impacts on our cultures, human and environmental health, human rights, well-being, traditional livelihoods, food systems and food sovereignty, local infrastructure, economic viability, and our very survival as Indigenous Peoples.

Mother Earth is no longer in a period of climate change, but in climate crisis. We therefore insist on an immediate end to the destruction and desecration of the elements of life.

Through our knowledge, spirituality, sciences, practices, experiences and relationships with our traditional lands, territories, waters, air, forests, oceans, sea ice, other natural resources and all life, Indigenous Peoples have a vital role in defending and healing Mother Earth. The future of Indigenous Peoples lies in the wisdom of our elders, the restoration of the sacred position of women, the youth of today and in the generations of tomorrow.

We uphold that the inherent and fundamental human rights and status of Indigenous Peoples, affirmed in the United Nations Declaration on the Rights of Indigenous Peoples (UNDRIP), must be fully recognized and respected in all decision-making processes and activities related to climate change. This includes our rights to our lands, territories, environment and natural resources as contained in Articles 25–30 of the UNDRIP. When specific programs and projects affect our lands, territories, environment and natural resources, the right of Self Determination of Indigenous Peoples must be recognized and respected, emphasizing our right to Free, Prior and Informed Consent, including the right to say "no". The United Nations Framework Convention on Climate Change (UNFCCC) agreements and principles must reflect the spirit and the minimum standards contained in UNDRIP. ∎

The full Anchorage Declaration can be accessed at:
www.indigenoussummit.com/servlet/content/declaration.html

However, without their even using the word 'green', green politics was advanced at Copenhagen as Latin American leaders from Cuba, Venezuela and, above all, Bolivia called for a new approach that puts respect for the Earth and social justice first. While it seems a little paradoxical that the leaders of states whose economy is based on oil (Venezuela under Hugo Chávez) or gas (Bolivia under Evo Morales), have called for radical cuts in carbon emissions, it is certainly to be welcomed.

Morales, the indigenous President of Bolivia, is a passionate advocate of radical green and anti-capitalist policies. He stunned the Copenhagen conference by insisting that rises in temperature must be limited to just one degree Celsius. Frustrated by the failure of Copenhagen, he has called for a global alliance of social movements to mobilize for real action on climate change, based on a new anti-capitalist economic model, respect for the Earth and a move towards global justice.

> 'Our objective is to save humanity and not just half of humanity. We are here to save Mother Earth. Our objective is to reduce climate change to [under] 1°C. [Above this] many islands will disappear and Africa will suffer a holocaust... The real cause of climate change is the capitalist system. If we want to save the earth then we must end that economic model. Capitalism wants to address climate change with carbon markets. We denounce those markets and the countries which [promote them]. It's time to stop making money from the disgrace that they have perpetrated.'[10]

In April 2010, he sponsored a conference of social movements and indigenous peoples aimed at building a global campaign of resistance, in Cochabamba, Bolivia. The first objective of the People's World Conference on Climate Change and Mother Earth's Rights – 'To analyze the structural and systemic causes that drive climate change and to propose radical measures to ensure the wellbeing of all humanity in harmony with nature'[11] – would seem to be a very good summary of what green politics is about. Indigenous people are increasingly making a green revolution and putting green politics into practice. The irony is that, while they don't use the green label, the color of their commitment is clear. The huge task ahead of green politics is likely to be re-energized by the work of indigenous leaders such as Morales. Perhaps the greatest hope for green politics comes at the moment from Latin America, but all of us, wherever we are, must struggle for green political change. Green politics is ultimately, after all, the politics of survival.

1 www.theecologist.info/page34.html 2 www.eco-action.org/dod/no6/rts.htm 3 Ted Trainer, 'The Transition Towns Movement; its huge significance and a friendly criticism', http://candobetter.org/node/1439 4 Paul Hawken, Hunter Lovins and Amory Lovins, *Natural Capitalism: Creating the Next Industrial Revolution*, Little Brown & Co, New York, 1999. 5 Jonathon Porritt, *Capitalism as if the World Matters*, Earthscan, London, 2007. 6 http://tinyurl.com/y8sjhf3 7 http://tinyurl.com/y9wkcyg 8 Alberto Melucci, *Challenging Codes: Collective Action in the Information Age*, Cambridge, 1996. 9 http://tinyurl.com/ybdgnp2 10 http://tinyurl.com/yd2kq9k 11 http://tinyurl.com/y8vh5wt

Bibliography

Books

Ian Angus, *The Global Fight for Climate Justice*, Resistance Books, London, 2009.

John Bellamy Foster, *The Ecological Revolution*, Monthly Review Press, New York, 2009.

Andrew Dobson, *Green Political Thought*, Routledge, London, 2007.

Whose Common Future/Reclaiming the Commons, The Ecologist, 1993.

Joel Kovel, *The Enemy of Nature*, Zed Press, London, 2002.

Jerry Mander, *Four Arguments for the Elimination of Television*, HarperPerennial, London, 1978.

Vandana Shiva, *Earth Democracy*, South End Press, New York, 2005.

Organizations and Green parties

International

Global Greens www.globalgreens.org/index.php

Indigenous Environmental Network www.ienearth.org/index.html

Ecosocialist International Network www.ecosocialistnetwork.org

Australia

The Australian Greens http://greens.org.au

Climate Camp www.climatecamp.org.au

Green Left www.greenleft.org.au

Canada

Green Party of Canada www.greenparty.ca

Ireland

Climate Camp www.climatecamp.ie

New Zealand/Aotearoa

Green Party of Aotearoa New Zealand www.greens.org.nz

United Kingdom

Green Party of England and Wales www.greenparty.org.uk

Scottish Green Party www.scottishgreens.org.uk

The Green Party in Northern Ireland www.greenpartyni.org

Climate Camp www.climatecamp.org.uk

United States

Green Party of the United States www.gp.org/index.php

Greenaction for Health & Environmental Justice www.greenaction.org

Index

Index

Index